What To Do When You're Depressed

What To Do When You're Depressed

A Christian Psychoanalyst Helps You
Understand and Overcome Your Depression

George A. Benson

AUGSBURG PUBLISHING HOUSE
Minneapolis, Minnesota

WHAT TO DO WHEN YOU'RE DEPRESSED

Copyright © 1975 Augsburg Publishing House

Library of Congress Catalog Card No. 75-22712

International Standard Book No. 0-8066-1519-2

Scripture quotations unless otherwise noted are from the Revised Standard Version of the Bible, copyright 1946, 1952, and 1971 by the Division of Christian Education of the National Council of Churches.

Manufactured in the United States of America

Dedicated to Anne, my wife, with thanks for her tireless assistance and loving criticism.

Contents

Introduction 9

I. Why Am I Depressed? 15
The Special Problems of Religious People
The Characteristics of Depression
Exhaustion
Everything Is Difficult and Tiring
Physical Symptoms
Illogical Logic
Summary

II. Depression: How Does It Work? 27
External Triggers
The Depressive Process
Depression Begins in Hope
Unexpressed Foolishness and Depression
Regression as a Way Out
Identification—"I'll Eat You Up."
Bad Food
A Deeper Look at Fatigue

III. The Emotional Hazards of Your Vacation 43
Operation Over-plan
"I Want to Be Free"
It Shouldn't Be This Good
Scapegoating
It's the Meaning of a Vacation that Counts
Don't Burn Down the House to Be Free

IV. Recreation: Let It Happen 58
"Total" Relaxation Is Hard Work
Nirvana Can Be Frightening
Canyons of Thought and Panic
Voices Out of Emptiness
De-escalation

V. I Dread Christmas 75
    The Happiness Bind
    The Christmas Setup
    Recapturing Childhood and Disillusionment
    The Failure of Success
    Deception and the Great Letdown
    Understanding Helps
    Imprisoned by "Good" Intentions

VI. Christmas Depressions for Young and Old 95
    Spare Us the Truth
    Christmas Shopping

VII. A Bundle of Joy and a Depression 111
    Depression May Be Unavoidable
    Natural Depression
    Life Can Be Beautiful—and Depressing
    Birth Is a Loss?
    Depression Is an Aspect of Growth

VIII. Depression and the Prime of Life 118
    Insight and Hard Work May Not Help
    Success Can Be Depressing
    Depression and the Middle-aged Kid

IX. Anniversaries, Birthdays—and Depression 126
    Meaningful Work vs. Meaningful People Who Work

X. Death: A Terminal Depression or Transcendent
   Growth 135

Introduction

I have written this book because I believe that much of the depression, unhappiness and emotional fatigue Christian people experience is unnecessary and avoidable. I also believe that when depression is unavoidable it may well become an important part of growth. Certainly I do not want to build up false optimism or present an unreal picture of human nature, but the truth is that many times people fall into useless and painful depression simply because they unwittingly accept a view of happiness based on the customs and demands of the world around them, rather than on an understanding of the private world within them.

Paradoxically, avoidable depression often strikes at times when we have every right to expect pleasure, relaxation, and celebration. Hence the reflective, Lenten times of life often bring us a disquieting sense of futility rather than a knowledge of Easter joy. The relaxation associated with vacations is often distorted by arguments and strain and Christmas may become a massive chore rather than an occasion for happiness and mirth.

We can rarely give expression to the unhappiness that is often and so unexpectedly associated with the holiday events of the year, but our concern is always with us. Much of the time it is felt as a blurred, inexplicable apprehension associated with pleasure. Sometimes it is experienced as a strange reluctance to anticipate happiness. Secretly we fear that our enthusiasm will become labored, our hopefulness will give way to a sense of "let-down," and our generosity will eventually leave us feeling "taken-in." Sooner or later we collect our fears under one umbrella and ask, "Why am I depressed when I am in the midst of occasions that promised joy?"

Because depression is not always avoidable let me make it clear that I cannot support a "boot-strap" concept of happiness and depression. It is important to make this clear since both basic Christian theology and good modern psychology force us to conclude that at times depression is quite natural. These are times when efforts to "snap out of it" just don't work. By the same token we are also led to conclude that these unavoidable days or weeks of depression may become an all important aspect of one's personal growth.

Generally speaking, unavoidable but growth-producing depression centers around those great natural events of life which bring us to a deeper realization of who we are and where we are going. For example, childbirth, a natural time for joy, is also a natural time for lifelong anxieties and doubts to emerge. This is probably why we are so intent on surrounding the event with an atmosphere of consistent happiness. In like manner, we spend much of our middle years, the prime of life, worrying about retirement and when retirement arrives we are apt to fear loneliness and death.

In dealing with unavoidable depression, I hope to clarify the fact that Christians who dare to understand the underlying psychological meaning of the great natural events of life need not be robbed of the knowledge and quiet pleasure of change any more than they need be deprived of the joyous sparkle of growth. For the Christian, these emotions are literally a right and reasonable reaction to a fuller knowledge of the creation of which they are a part.

In summary, let me say that a lifelong love of the church, (a love that is sometimes tempered with disappointment and pain), supports my psychiatric conviction that depression, a problem which is of intimate importance to us all, must never be dealt with simplistically. Nevertheless, my desire to write this book stems from my personal knowledge that occasions that are meant to be joyful can indeed be alive with festivity and celebration. And, even though every thoughtful person must experience periods of depression that are a part of growth, we need not settle for a rationalized, melancholic view of human nature. We need not artificially comfort ourselves with the unreal psychologies of those who tell us that our basic nature can be freed of perversity and conflict nor need we accept the notion that the truth about ourselves is so brutalizing that it can only lead to faithless, secular "realism."

Finally, let me make it clear that failure to respond to this book does not mean that you have not tried, or believed or trusted hard enough. It does not mean that you must berate yourself or throw yourself open to the endless questions and suggestions of well-meaning friends who are convinced that they have a hammerlock on happiness. In this regard, the world of popular psychological writing can be cruel. At times, authors imply that their books can alleviate the pain associated with almost any psychological problem. Often these authors go on to suggest that they have already helped "countless thousands" and so the reader feels compelled to respond. Of course, such an attitude is insufferably pompous, but more importantly, when this approach is taken to the subject of depression the writer may inflict a tragic sense of failure on people who already suffer more anguish than they can bear; people who need more help than they can get from any book because their depression is the result of unconscious forces that cannot be examined without professional help.

No one wants to believe that they are the victim of powerful emotions and ideas which they cannot control by deliberate thought. As a matter of fact, most of us not only find this idea difficult to believe, we may find it frightening and even maddening. Nevertheless, it is true that sometimes aspects of our personality which we would most like to change are due to convictions and emotions, thoughts and feelings which we cannot fathom by ourselves. Authors who appeal to our desire to believe that we can be complete masters of our own mind simply deceive us. And when deception prolongs human suffering it is not clever, it is cruel. If this is difficult for the Christian reader to accept, let me point out that what I am saying is very much in the mainstream of Christian theology. Christians have never had any reason to believe that they can be completely knowledgeable about themselves and therefore in charge of themselves. As a matter of fact, I would go a step further and say that any Christian who trusts God to be accepting and helpful of just those aspects of themselves which they know about practices a shallow faith. No one knew better than St. Paul that God has to be trusted to accept, to love and redeem aspects of oneself which makes us do that which we would not do and keep us from doing that which we would do.

Plainly speaking, this is a book of clearly stated, illustrated facts and suggestions meant to help people who suffer needlessly with depression that can be resolved by understanding; depression that can either be avoided or made a creative part of growth. At one time or another we all suffer from this kind of depression.

Aside from facts and suggestions derived from facts, I can only offer the reader the healing perspective of humor. Depression and the debilitating pain that characterizes it is the only serious psychological problem that touches us all at one time or another. It is far too serious to be left to facts and understanding alone. So you will occasionally find something amusing in this book. There will be occasions to enjoy humor that sets tragedy in its place with a smile.

I

Why Am I Depressed?

Just what is depression? Because most people recognize depression as a feeling or emotion it's really very hard for them to say just what it is. Describing an emotion is like describing a color. So to ask what is depression is like asking what is the color red. People who are depressed are usually acutely aware of how hard it is for them to describe their condition and this is one of the reasons why they feel so isolated. They have to struggle with fuzzy phrases like "I'm feeling blue," "I'm down in the mouth," or "What's the use of living?"

The Special Problems of Religious People

Depression which at best takes all the fun out of life and at worst absorbs one in continuous gloomy preoccupations, is a common condition of all people at one time or another. Religious people, however, have some particular trouble in both owning up to and expressing depression. It is often difficult for them to admit being depressed because they consider it to be a sign of a lack of faith.

Modern Christians have been raised on the conviction that Christ always loves and always accepts. From this apparently liberating concept they either consciously or unconsciously conclude that they have no "legitimate" cause to be depressed. Such men and women are apt to be swept off their feet when they must go through a period of depression, during which being loved and accepted is painful, if not intolerable. The Apostle Peter knew how terrible it could be to be accepted by Christ, but modern Christians often assume that things should at least be "OK" if not "fantastic" just because they are accepted. To them, "down" feelings are a sure indication that their spiritual life is out of order. Sincere Christian people do not always have their beliefs and assumptions in clear, conscious focus. They may not realize that they equate depression with faithlessness, but they usually do. And then the problem of depression is all the more difficult to solve.

In this regard I am reminded of a young Christian who became depressed shortly after he had been relocated and given a management position in one of his company's branch offices. It was the job he had always wanted. It was his "chance of a lifetime," and he expected to enjoy it. Although he came to me voluntarily for professional help, it was six months before he was able to share with me his "terrible feelings of endless loneliness, helplessness, and unwarranted anger." When he finally did express these feelings, he had to add a sense of spiritual failure to his list of painful emotions.

To this formerly eager, enthusiastic young man, depression meant that he had lost his faith. After all, Christ loved him so why should he not be joyful? "Why," he asked, "should I be so shaken by the alienation I feel from the people in my company, my friends, and my loved ones? Why should it get me down so?" He was so hung up with the sense of failure and hurt these questions caused him that it took him a long time before he could bring himself to tell me that as a result of his depression he had become rigidly righteous in his professional life, unloving in his married life, and punitive in his intimate thinking about himself. Tragically, his denial of his depression had turned his probationary year as a manager into a nightmare of confusion and self-doubt which could not be shared and hence could not be worked out. Now, in all good conscience, he could not go ahead with his most creative plans and so he had a depressing secondary problem which loomed even larger and weighed even heavier than his initial depression. He was mediocre in a job in which he intended to excel.

The Characteristics of Depression

There are a number of things that can be seen in this situation besides the unhappy result of holding depression inside of oneself for fear that expressing it would expose faithless fears. First of all, our description of depression is enlarged by this man's experience of "terrible feelings of endless loneliness, helplessness and petty anger." Let's consider these adjectives one at a time.

Endlessness

In my experience, depression of any magnitude carries with it a sense of endlessness. It is typical of depressed people to feel that their condition will never cease. As a result they see little or no sense in "trying." Often it's a great effort even to say, "What's the use?", or "So I'm a failure, O.K., I admit it, and what's more I don't care." Past accomplishments are little support. Rather than a foundation upon which present day actions may be based, they evaporate and appear to have been moments of self-deception. When the "blues" hit, there appears to be no future worth planning for. Ideas which just a week before were clear and bright enough to give purpose and aim to one's future, become clouded over with doubt and anxiety. And it's all endless. Even though the sufferer may have felt the pain of depression on many previous occasions and even though he may have recovered from a number of bouts with the condition in the past, the present experience feels hopeless, unrelenting and incurable. *Endlessness is a characteristic of depression.*

Loneliness Gets Worse with Help

It goes without saying that loneliness is a characteristic of depression but it is not obvious that the loneliness of depression is usually intensified by the efforts of well-intentioned friends and relatives to bridge the gap between themselves and their depressed loved one. Concerned persons cannot and must not give up their attempt to make contact, but unless they understand the true nature of depression the chances that they will be a source of lasting relief are minimal. Even when the uninformed layman's encouragement and support seem to have lightened the depressive burden a little, it is usually only a short time until the old loneliness has re-exerted itself. Sometimes it returns with vengeance and what little normal communications existed are silenced. With this turn of events depressed persons are in great danger for unless they are fortunate enough to be attended by a friend possessed of insight and patience, they are liable to end up in a state of external "real" loneliness rather than with just a painful "feeling" of loneliness. This happens because the depressed men or women who cry out for relief from their loneliness will more than likely attract the attention of well-meaning people who will give of themselves only to recoil when their initial success backfires. *Ironically, depressive loneliness usually leads to more loneliness.*

Helplessness

It is this kind of negative reaction to well-meaning efforts that leads many, if not most, non-depressed people to believe that depression can be shrugged off or disciplined away if the victim really wants to get over it. Trying to help, only to find one's efforts producing more pain, is the kind of experience that will disappoint and probably anger most would-be helpers. Hence, they find themselves saying something foolish like, "Come on and snap out of it," or "When are you going to stop playing games." The important thing to realize here is that most of this reaction stems from the hurt feelings and frustrations of the well-intentioned people who tried to help. These reactions do not represent an understanding of depression. An understanding of depression would include an emphatic realization of the *helplessness* felt by the depressed person. Depressed people feel driven to be alienating, and to be alienated. For example, a non-depressed mother may say "I can't stand my kids today, I've got to get away from them!" But a depressed mother feels driven to say the same thing hurtfully, i.e. in front of the children.

It is true that depressed persons regret the pain they mete out to others but most of the time their outbursts only result in more depression; more bad feelings about themselves. They can't stop. And, of course, these feelings of self-hate and loathing will eventually break loose and produce another hurtful scene. In all of this the observer feels willfully pushed out and misused by sufferers who could "cut it out" any time they felt like it. The victims, however, are filled with a sense of helplessness. They understand the illogic of their thoughts and actions but their feelings follow an ancient logic that defies the mature intellect.

Anger and the Downward Spiral

The last part of the description bears particular attention. The young executive said, "I feel unwarranted, petty, anger." After a while he loosened up a little more and then he put it this way, "I seem to hate the people closest to me, the ones I love the most. Just when things are going good, I feel anger descending on me. I feel overcome. I know I'm hurting people and blaming them for things they didn't mean to do but I can't help it. I just hate them." As he described his predicament to me it was obvious that he was angry about getting angry. I was relieved to hear this expression of anger because it reassured me that my patient was not so far gone into the depressive cycle that he had reached the conclusion that his anger was just a new proof of his worthlessness. Many people never dare admit that with their depression they are very, very angry. These people realize that their anger makes little or no sense to anyone except themselves and since they can't trust themselves they set it aside. As a result the depression is much more difficult to unwind. It takes a much longer time to get over.

Here again, I suppose religious people have a more difficult time working with depression. While most Christian denominations have dropped the preceding generation's out-of-hand rejection of anger, few Christians are able to listen to the "unwarranted" anger of a depressed person with equanimity. After all, Christ said "Forgive them" when he was hurt and rejected and since we are to be like Christ, there seems to be no room for depressive anger. We too should be forgiving. The problem with this assumption is that it entails copying and imitating Christ rather than accepting the maturing process which, among other things, one sees exemplified in the life of Christ. More of this in Chapter Two. The anger of depression is just like the loneliness of depression in that it takes on a self-fulfilling quality. That is, the more one holds anger inside because one sees it as a stupid and humiliating emotion, the more it is apt to break out in a hurtful way; and the more hurtful one is the more worthless one feels.

So depressed persons enter into a downward spiral which usually ends with their replacing expressions of anger with, "Go away, just let me alone." What the sufferer is really saying is, "Go away, can't you understand that anything I say will come out in a way that will only prove how bad I am? Let me alone while I can still stand myself."

In the next chapter I will consider this self-fulfilling prophecy aspect of depression in greater depth. We must try to get at some of its real causes, but for now, it is important for us to realize that anger that is felt to be inappropriate either because it's directed at the "wrong" person or because it is "overdone" is a part of depression. It does little or no good to speak to the anger alone. Neither forgiveness, explanations or rebuttal help very much. One must deal with the depressive picture as a whole. Futile, apparently unwarranted anger is an important part of that picture.

Exhaustion

Depression, however, may present itself in an entirely different way. An active career woman and mother of three children described "a feeling of utter exhaustion whenever I try to do anything. I used to have trouble getting to sleep. Now I have trouble staying awake. I feel as if I've been drugged." When depression appears in this form, it may be easily mistaken for the fatigue of working too hard. This mistake is particularly easy to make when the depression is not intense; when the sufferer simply feels chronically tired.

But there are other symptoms of depression which accompany this condition and which make it diagnosable by the layman.

Among married couples, for example, one of the first signs that one or the other partner is depressed is a "tired" attitude toward married love life. The man or woman who habitually says "not tonight, dear. I'm too tired," or "I've got a headache," is probably depressed. There are some good indications that Christian people are now taking sex seriously, i.e. they are beginning to see sex as an honest-to-God important part of life. But it is still hard for many middle-aged and older people to seek help because lovemaking drops off to once a month. Their sense of worthlessness and fatigue almost forces them to conclude that their time for love and ecstasy is over. Ironically, it may be particularly difficult for them when they turn to a "good Christian doctor" for help. One such doctor told a former patient of mine who had turned to him for help in overcoming her problem with constant disinterest and lack of satisfaction, "Just try to forget it and soon you'll learn to get along without it." When the patient asked, "But what about my husband?" the doctor said, "If it really bothers him, I suggest that you learn how to pretend that he is satisfying you."

If all of this sounds a little primitive and unlikely to you, let me assure you that it is not. It is especially true for Christian couples past fifty. *It is appalling how many middle-aged people find time to spend six to twelve hours at church working on this or that committee, board, or guild, only to find themselves too exhausted for love.* And the whole process is more than likely sanctified by the authoritative word of priest, minister or doctor.

Of course, making love is not limited to sexuality. People whose depression takes a tired and passive form are also estranged from other forms of love. The kids who used to be fun on occasion are now mostly "too demanding and too much work." Of course, this is not always true. Sometimes the children are used just as church may be used, i.e. as a means by which one rationalizes the relentless fatigue that has smothered spontaneous love of all forms.

Everything Is Difficult and Tiring

One of the most interesting and noticeable features of depression is the victim's peculiar inability to enjoy things. It is as if a "lead hand" pushes one down to the ground whenever the possibility of pleasure appears. Everything is oppressively difficult.

I can never forget the first time I encountered this condition. A young friend and I had planned for weeks to spend the first Saturday after our graduation from high school just bumming around downtown Chicago. We arranged to meet by the bronze lions in front of the Art Museum. The day and appointed time arrived. I was there but my friend was not. An hour and a half later I caught sight of him trudging up Michigan Avenue looking as if he had not slept for a week. But his initial apology corrected my misimpression. "Sorry, I'm late," he said, "but I simply overslept." I was ready to forget the incident but I knew something was really wrong when my friend fell into a torpid silence broken only by complaints. "I wonder why the entrance isn't on the ground level, then you wouldn't have to walk up so many steps." "Look at that picture," (it was Reuben's "The Chastisement of Innocence"), "just think of how much work it took to get all those details down." To him, the sparkling white Wrigley Tower was remarkable only because "somebody had to wash it all the time." The highlight of the day for me was to have been a visit to the Chicago Historical Society but we never got there. My friend decided to call it a day while he could still get a bus that would take him straight home without having to transfer.

I was too young to know that my friend was depressed but I certainly knew that there was something very wrong. *He experi-*

*enced everything we had intended to enjoy in terms of work,
effort, and fatigue.*

Physical Symptoms

The last obvious form of depression to be considered in this
chapter is depression which is characterized by physical symptoms.
I must make it clear at the onset that it is very dangerous to conclude that a physical symptom is caused by depression without
first having had a complete medical check-up. To the untrained
eye, physical symptoms caused by depression are identical to physical symptoms caused by physical problems and vice-versa. *Depression can mimic almost any kind of physical problem.* Headaches,
backaches, loss of appetite, stomach upset, and bowel trouble; dys-
menorrhea, insomnia, fatigue and stiff neck, are all symptoms
which *may* be caused by depression. One of the things which
may give the layman a hint that depression is the basic cause of
physical symptoms is the pessimistic view patients hold toward
their symptoms. Everything seems to be an indication of decay
and the approach of death. Some people are dramatic in their
expression of pessimism and some people are very quiet; but
when physical symptoms are caused by depression, the sufferer is
oppressed by a sense of doom and gloom. One should suspect
that physical symptoms have a depressive root when there is
physical relief that corresponds with an upswing in mood and
an increase in symptoms when there is a downturn in mood.

Illogical Logic

Obviously depression is more than a bad feeling or a painful
emotion. Perhaps the single most important characteristic of
depression is its illogical logic. Depression is a state of mind in

which joy makes no sense and pessimism seems logical. When one is depressed, happy thoughts, plans and actions may appear to be positively irrational. They appear to be a frivolous waste of time. The whole thrust of life is toward defeat, discouragement, failure and meaninglessness. If depression involved nothing more than unhappiness then people probably could "snap out of it" the way one is told to do by nondepressed friends. Unfortunately, even minor depressions include a distortion of the intellectual processes which makes a depressive attitude appear to be both reasonable and appropriate.

I will always remember a young man who turned to me for help with a depression that began shortly after he had been awarded a full graduate scholarship to one of the great English universities. The scholarship was an opportunity of a lifetime, but by the time he came to me he had already turned it down. Emotionally, everything about the venture seemed to be too exhausting, too much work, and too lonely. To him these were entirely appropriate emotions. Intellectually, the whole project simply didn't make sense. He reasoned that since his father was a truck driver, his mother "just a housewife," and his five brothers and sisters were never going to make it through high school, he would be an outcast from his family for the rest of his life if he moved ahead toward a Ph.D. in philosophy. He was certain that the only fair, honest, and "reasonable" thing to do was to stay home and get a job. His thinking was crystallized by the simple arithmetic of wages. He had calculated that as a university professor, the profession he really wanted, he would be 40 years old before he had made as much money as he would if he were to discontinue his education and take a job with his father's firm. His talent for philosophy, his genuine desire to be a teacher and his parents' obvious hope that he would be the one person in the family that would break out of the world of labor which, while they respected it, limited their own lives; all of this made no sense to him. In his depressed mood, the only logic he could accept was the logic of money and physical security, for these were the only things that offered relief from his depression. Everything associated with adventure and pleasure seemed to be an exercise in futility.

Unhappily this young man's depressive emotions were frozen in place by his depressive logic. I could not help him. He gave up his chance of a lifetime because the *illogical logic of a transient depression* won the day and thus changed the course of his entire life.

Summary

In summary, let me point out that I have tried to do two things in this first chapter. The major portion has been devoted to a description of the emotional aspects of depression. I have emphasized the emotions of depression since they are the easiest way to recognize depression in oneself and in others. And since one cannot change a condition that is not recognized for what it is, it is of the utmost importance that we learn to see depression as a painful emotional state that appears to be endless, and appears to warrant a foreclosure on the joy of life. I have closed the chapter with a short exposition of the intellectual distortion that occurs in depression because without an understanding of the apparent "reasonableness" of depression, one is helplessly locked into it. The logic of depression destroys one's motivation for change because it creates a perspective from which change appears to be both unnecessary and impossible to achieve.

II

Depression:
How Does It Work?

If we are to understand depression so that we need not be baffled by it, we must broaden our knowledge to include its inner workings: the means by which it overcomes us. And if this is to be a fruitful search for knowledge, then it is of primary importance that we start with the realization that depression is not just a response to "depressing" circumstances. It does indeed have an inner personal way of overtaking us. Unless one is severely depressed, one usually blames the condition on something external but an objective look at the things people blame for their depressed feelings does not clarify the situation. Indeed, many of the situations people find depressing are meant to be joyful.

External Triggers

Sometimes we think that the actions of a loved one or a friend account for our depression, but to an objective observer there appears to be no reason for us to be depressed. The observer may see good reasons for discouragement or sadness but not for depression. This is not to say that the external observer is right and the depressed sufferer is wrong. As a matter of fact, they are both right. The observer is right because usually there are no obvious reasons for depression, and the victim is right, not because it is correct to account for depression in terms of external problems, but because the victim intuitively realizes that very small things that others may not notice can take on enormously important personal meaning. Depressed people are incorrect when they try to account for their problem entirely in terms of the world around them, but potential helpers are quite wrong when they do not recognize the triggering effect of the external world.

A man who turned to me for help with his depression was quite correct in dating the onset of the "blues" at 5:45 P.M. on Friday, two months before our first appointment. It was at that moment that he discovered that one of his children had the measles, thus preventing his wife from joining him on a week's business holiday. He was even correct in accounting for the onset of his mild depression in terms of the way his wife broke the news to him. "It was her matter-of-fact appraisal of the situation that really got to me." He was grossly in error, however, when he failed to realize that this disappointment did not in itself warrant two months of "lousy feelings." It was a trigger for a whole process of thinking which, after it had been brought into play, went on quite independently of the external situation that started it. Actually, this man was able to postpone his business trip for several weeks, but by then he had lost interest. In a matter-of-fact way very reminiscent of the manner he found so depressing in his wife, he said, "There's no use in going. We'd just spend a lot of money and besides, I couldn't show her a good time now anyhow."

Sometimes the triggering event is even less noticeable than this.

A loved one's oversight, or failure to smile; a child's selfishness; a phrase in the pastor's sermon; soup on a favorite necktie; a dress that doesn't hang right; the honking of an impatient motorist; all may be an introduction to "down" feelings that might go on independently for days afterwards. And, of course, sometimes depression might start without an external trigger. Sometimes one's own thoughts or impulses, even though they are never carried into action, can be the impetus for the depressive process.

The Depressive Process

Just what is the depressive process? Let's consider depression that is summed up by the statement, "I'm no good, no one can love me." Later we will take a deeper look at depression that is expressed with the statement, "What's the use, I'm too tired. I just don't have the energy." The best way to describe complicated psychological processes in adults is to observe children, because children will usually show us the same process in simple and obvious ways. A few years ago, my family and I were invited to a party at which there were four adult couples and six or eight children ranging in age from six to twelve years old. For the most part the adults were too engaged with each other to worry about the kids, but occasionally one of us would put in a parental, "Let's keep it quiet." However, one middle-aged mother was more than a little upset by the din of childish laughter, squabbles and games. She constantly nagged her daughter, an eight-year-old, to "Quiet down," "Don't run," and "Are you sure Mrs. Johnson (our hostess) said you could play with that ball?" Since the child's father had died in an auto accident just six months before this incident, one would expect that she was still a sad and lonely little girl. But when she turned to her mother for attention, all she got was another admonition. Of course, the less successful the girl was in winning some form of affection from her mother, the more frantically she tried.

As the evening wore on, her play became more and more intense; her demands for attention became incessant. Finally a crisis was reached. The girl kicked a large rubber ball right at a family portrait on the mantle. With this, the mother unleashed a burst of verbal sarcasm, "How could you be so stupid!" etc. She ended her little diatribe with a hard slap on the culprit's bottom. The whole incident took only a few minutes and soon the party was back in full swing. The child, however, did not return to her play. One would expect that an average child would be quiet for a while only to return shortly to its activity on a somewhat attenuated scale. But such was not the case with this little girl. She moved quietly out of the living room to a bedroom where I caught sight of her sitting on the floor behind a door, sucking her thumb like a two-year-old baby. Soon enough her mother found her, but contrary to my expectations, she did not scold her daughter. Instead she smiled, a little sternly, reached out her hand and escorted her daughter back to the living room. Once there, the child was a different person. At the close of the evening her mother put it this way, "Why, she's been a perfect little lady all evening."

Behaviorwise she was indeed a perfect lady after her run-in with her mother. Her eyes, however, told me that she was also a sad "little lady." The life went out of her. She talked very little and when she did it was to express the same kind of exasperation and criticism we had come to expect from her mother. In other words, she had adopted her mother's outlook. Now she was irritated and angry with herself in the same way her mother was angry with her. In a sense she became her mother. I found out later that she was bored with school and often too tired to play out of doors with the other children. She was often sick and complained almost all of the time about almost everything. Why was this little girl depressed at the age of eight?

Depression Begins in Hope

Like all of the people we have thus far mentioned, she was, at the time depression struck, needy and looking for attention. Like the eager young executive who looked forward to his first independent job and like the businessman who anticipated the week away from home with his wife, this girl was expectant. The reasons for expectancy may differ, but the point is that depression begins with an attitude of longing, wishfulness and hope. The hope that is actually expressed may seem modest and appropriate. The fulfillment one says one desires may be entirely reasonable. The young executive's hope for a close relationship with his staff and the businessman's desire for a vacation with his wife were both quite realistic. But what these people did not express, not even to themselves, was a desire for gratification that would be complete; utterly blissful. What they actually wanted was Camelot. The situation that started their depression had become highly charged with desires that were ordinarily hidden and satisfied in covert ways. So when frustration hit it shattered dreams and crushed hopes that were way out of proportion to the actual situation.

Frustration is always difficult to take but depression only follows the frustration of unspoken hopes and dreams that are the hub of one's hopefulness about life itself. The important thing to remember is that more often than not it is the small things in life that attract such hopes. The intimate details of life are most often the vehicles upon which our deepest and most basic hopes ride. And so it is often the apparently small frustrations that shatter us and introduce despair. One of the major reasons that depression is so poorly understood and one of the major reasons why we are so victimized by it is the fact that we do not understand that it begins with a state of yearning which is usually unrealized and unexpressed, and this yearning often centers on small but highly symbolic acts and events which take on a life or death importance.

Whether or not depression follows frustration also depends on the general state of one's mind at the time of frustration. Fatigue, hunger, illness, etc., may reduce our ability to pass over a charged frustration and thus it becomes a trigger for depression. And, as we shall see later, there are times in everyone's life when we are set up for depression because we are almost forced into a state of fatigued hopefulness.

Unexpressed Foolishness and Depression

This first step in understanding depression raises an important question that must be asked and answered before we go on to a further understanding of our subject. Why don't people express their intimate hopes and wishes? Why are they so often hidden even from themselves? And why does this happen in a Christian community that supposedly thrives on the total acceptance of God and of each other? The answer is quite simple. However reasonable we may try to make our private, basic wishes appear, (I'm speaking of the kind of wishes that lead us into depression when they are frustrated) they are in fact founded on the cherished illusions of childhood. At heart we all hope for unquestioning love, endless nourishment, and unearned security.

Now our questions can be asked in a more specific way. Why can't people express these foolish but fundamentally important hopes of childhood? Why does every hope and desire have to be pushed into an appearance of rational maturity before it can be owned up to? Why do some people have to be intoxicated before they can take their natural fancifulness seriously? Why must some people force themselves to interpret their babylike desires for closeness as sexual and thereby either reject or experience them in an "adult" frame of reference? Why do so many young people have to turn to drugs before they can believe in the desires and hopes of youth? More specifically, how can the Christian community that includes among its progenitors James and John, who in a burst of presumptuous infantile desire, asked to be seated on the right and left hand of God; how can this community be unaccepting of the private hopes and dreams of mankind? Are some churches growing in size and influence because they still welcome wishful thinking and passionately hopeful believing?

The highly rational as well as the social theologies of the twentieth century are great advances, but insofar as they stifle our ability to listen sensitively to the childlike desires we all feel, they are an incalculable setback. Any theological stance that fosters maturity, social responsibility, and right action in opposition to an expression of private foolishness, simply steels itself against the substance of joy and miracles. It invites depression.

Yet this is what often happens. Christian men and women will get together on any project that can be made to look "sensible." They can get together on anything that appears to be "reasonable," and "appropriate." But let one bad breath drunk wander into church (they don't much anymore) and shout "Hallelujah!" and they are shattered. How dare he penetrate our calculated facade and express our stifled joy? "Call the cops. He's disturbing our peace." Many Christian churches today prefer to be mature, (that means we have meetings, lots and lots of meetings and plans of action) and depressed (that means we are "realistic") rather than let the childish, foolish, light of human nature shine through our self-induced darkness.

Regression as a Way Out

Now let's get back to our depressed little girl. You remember that after her hopes for some attention had been thoroughly frustrated, she crawled off to a corner in another room and began to suck her thumb like a baby. This is a complex bit of behavior that has been discussed in volumes of professional literature and yet, because it is a basic part of almost any depression, it is essential that we break it down and discuss it in conversational language. The first thing the child did was to seek isolation. To the casual observer, the reason seems obvious. She had been hurt and wanted to be left alone. Of course, there are times when we all need to be alone in order to get things sorted out, soothe our feelings, and take a second look at our problems. But notice that when our subject retreated into isolation she also transformed herself into a very little girl. She actually became an infant in every non-physical way. Now she was no longer a rejected little girl who had suffered a hurtful loss of hope; a loss of her strained belief that mother was indeed the ever-warm and helping person she wanted her to be. Now she was a hungry baby who needed nourishment and so she sucked her thumb. Of course her thumb was only a symbol for her mother. It was a symbol for her mother as she knew her years ago when life was "good." In other words, if she couldn't have her mother as an eight-year-old she would have her as a baby.

Now we must examine the question, just how do babies "have" their mother? It is qualitatively different from the way an eight-year-old or an adult relates to mother. An eight-year-old can play, or learn or run errands or just give a big hug to be loved; i.e. to "have" mother. But an infant can do none of these things. An infant can do only one thing really well. An infant can eat. It is the act of nourishment through which an infant loves and is loved. It is by taking things into the mouth that babies explore the world.

Identification — "I'll Eat You Up."

Babies learn and grow and become individuals by incorporation. In this sense an infant literally drinks its mother in and while it does, it becomes one with her, fused with her. Hence the frantic cry of the child that awakens from a long nap and finds itself hungry. The cry is more than a plea for food, although given the child's helplessness this too can be urgent. The frantic nature of the hungry child's cry stems from the realization of aloneness. And as any parent knows, a child can be satisfied for a long period of time by being held and rocked. The satisfaction comes from the closeness, not from nourishment. In like manner, older children suck their thumb when they are frightened, alone, and in need of comfort. Thumbsucking is rarely just a bad habit. Most of the time it is a sign of loneliness that can only be overcome by reverting to the frame of reference of infancy; the frame of reference in which "I am hers and she is mine because I have taken her inside of me." In other words, our little girl actually took her mother inside of her, she became like her in order to overcome the separation she felt when she tried to relate to her mother as a mature eight-year-old. (Remember we said she began to complain just like her mother.)

In some respects we take parts or aspects of people into ourselves all of our lives in order to avoid a total loss of them. Students adopt some of the important ways of thinking of a beloved professor after graduation. In this way the professor literally lives on in the student's life. Children go back to the religious faith of their parents in times of stress and thus feel the closeness of lost loved ones again. But of course the most profound example of all is the Christian eucharistic feast. Although the ceremony has many levels of meanings, its deepest psychological meaning is only perceived when we realize that at the core of our nature there is the infant's yearning to become one with the sustainer of life by incorporating the substance of life. To eat the body and blood of Christ is to become one with Christ. It is the most basic means we know of overcoming the loneliness of life; of having the love of God within us.

Bad Food

But these are good, affirmative examples of incorporation. If we incorporate a lost "loved one" everything is fine, the sense of loss is overcome. It is true that for a while our life is not quite our own. Men and women who have lost their spouse find themselves doing, saying and thinking things that are indeed an expression of the personality of the lost loved one. But sooner or later these characteristics are sorted out and we retain the ones which symbolically keep us in touch with the lost person but which do not pre-empt our own way of life.

To understand our little girl, to understand depression, we must ask one more question. What happens if the lost loved one is also a lost hated one? This is what happened to our eight-year-old. She loved her mother. She yearned to be close to her but she was rejected. Insofar as she wanted to be lovingly close to a loving mother, she lost her mother. And in her frustration and loss she hated her mother. Now she wanted to be close but the only way to be close was to adopt her mother's anger. When she crawled off into the corner, became an infant and sucked her thumb, she had to invent a way to be close to an angry mother who rejected her. And so she became like her mother. She literally incorporated her mother's rejecting attitude. And this is the anatomy of depression. A man or woman who has just received communion should feel affirmed and strengthened. It is as if there is a voice inside saying, "All is well, I am with you and I love you." But when we feel rejected by a loved one, when we symbolically swallow up a loved one with whom we are angry, there is a voice inside saying, "You are bad, you are evil." We are close to the rejecting loved one because we are angry with ourselves in the same way the loved one was angry with us. In other words, we share rejection. Hence a war that was once carried on between two people is now painfully contained within the confines of one head. In the truest sense of the word, depressed people are divided against themselves. They are divided between themselves and the frustrating person they have taken into themselves in the hope of avoiding the pain of separation.

One can always maneuver around a frustrating person. But how can one get around that person when it has become a voice within oneself; when it has become part of oneself? One cannot. When we are frustrated with life, we might say, "To hell with it all." But depressed people cannot separate themselves from the frustration of life. They have taken that frustration within themselves. In a desperate attempt to avoid loneliness they have become a frustrator.

This is why depressed persons feel "there is no use in living." They feel as though they can never get free of hate because the object of their hate is now inside of them. It has become part of themselves; it is self-hate. People who try to help by saying, "Cheer up, you have everything to live for," are completely *unhelpful.* Depressed people are so close to the muzzle of hatred they can see no way of escape. In order to avoid separation, they have taken into themselves the characteristics of the one to whom they've wanted to be close. They have become the person they yearn to be near. Unfortunately, that person was an angry rejector.

Before I close this chapter with two short examples of this process, let me remind you just why I am spending so much time on this subject. Self-hate is the most important and the most unique characteristic of depression. Depressed people may express their anger with themselves in different terms but it boils down to self-hate. In other words, unless this aspect of depression is understood we will miss the whole point of the book, i.e. to do something about depression. Without exploring the process of psychologically overcoming separation by taking into oneself the "rejecting," "hurtful" attitude of the person one hoped to be close to, this could only be a book on discouragement. The workings of self-hate must be understood if we are to understand depression.

A little boy named John went through this cycle when his father cancelled a fishing trip and went off on business without any explanation. The boy was rejected and so he regressed, i.e. he lost his grip on the level of maturity he had attained. But to everyone's surprise "he came out of it," and seemed to be "mother's little man." First, fear and loneliness forced this child backwards. For an hour, a day or a week he went back to clutching a security blanket and then the magic happened. He emerged from his childish regression acting "for all the world like his father." As such, the boy felt less separated and less alone. Now he had something in common with the absent father. In part, he had become his father. He had taken his father's characteristic rejection into himself. He created a sense of closeness that surpassed mere daydreams and blotted out the fear of lonely separation.

But what about his anger at his father for leaving? That didn't go away. It simply got redirected. The child became the father and so the child was now rejecting of himself. To his unsuspecting mother this looked like precocious maturity; an unusual capacity to be self-regulating and self-critical. She expected angry tears and pouting, but what she got was a day or two of babyish regression followed by days of boyish, clever attempts to be like his father. Now he denounced the fishing trip he had once hoped to enjoy. But to John it was an exhausting process of impossible imitation fraught with failure and self-hate. He hated his father for leaving but since he was trying to overcome loneliness by being like his father he had to be rejecting of himself. Tragically, he became depressed. He felt worthless and unloveable; his effort to avoid separation led to an intolerable internal division.

In order to apply these examples to adult life we need only keep in mind the idea that depression is triggered by small things which, given the way we honestly and privately look at the world, are symbolically important to us. Remember that the things which trigger depression may appear to be very unimportant to the external observer. What really counts is what these triggering situations, ideas or events mean to the individual who gets depressed. Hence, a middle-aged preacher's wife who was bored with housework and wanted to get a part-time, paying job ended up depressed. Her husband not only rejected the idea of his wife getting a job, he unwittingly rejected his wife's unspoken desire to feel useful and loved. The rejection was too subtle and righteous for her to combat. The threatened isolation was too much to risk and so she became like her husband. When she saw me she was righteously depreciating of her desire to get out of the house. She hated her own idea. She was depressed.

A Deeper Look at Fatigue

Now let's consider for a moment depression characterized by a sense of fatigue. It is an internal sense of helplessness; a sense of exhaustion and of being overwhelmed, that gives one that feeling of "what's the use," which, along with the feeling, "I'm no good, no one can love me," characterize the core of depression. A closer look at this sense of uselessness shows us that it is always experienced in relation to a failure to realize highly idealistic aspirations. A closer look is necessary because often these idealistic aspirations are extremely private. They may be disguised by a great deal of rationalized thought about ordinary objectives and one's failure to achieve them.

This is a particularly important aspect of depression for Christian people to understand because the expectations religious people have for themselves are so intimately connected with their personal theology. Religious people find it extremely difficult to face what they are and live with what they can be. They find it compellingly attractive to bewail what they are and strive toward what they "should" be.

Before I elaborate on this statement, it must be made clear that this tendency is not peculiar to the Christian church. Whenever people band together in formal groups they tend to sort out those characteristics which they believe to be more acceptable than others. Even groups of "do your own thing," freedom lovers are selective. People who won't or can't give up old ways of thinking and behaving are eventually unwelcome in these so-called utterly accepting groups.

Christian theology strongly affirms the idea that the grace of God is large enough to include any and all people irrespective of their personal characteristics. Unfortunately depression does not depend on this theology. It does not depend on God's acceptance and forgiveness, *but on one's own acceptance of the fact that God is accepting.* Unhappily, Christian morality is all too often taught without helping people see that there is a clear distinction between what one does and should do and what one is and might be. We should feel charitable but we might very well be angry. We should demonstrate our love but we might in fact feel hurt and pain. The Christian faith might and should offer us an unsurpassed opportunity to know that we are loved irrespective of what we have done, thought or felt; irrespective of what we are. Because love that passes all understanding overcomes the dread of separation, the depressive process need never start. Rejection only leads to imitation, self-hate, depression and the ultimate sin: alienation.

Unfortunately this theological truth is often distorted into "God loves you, therefore you should be loving, virtuous, kind, etc." This in itself is not too bad but usually the distortion goes on until it implies non-acceptance if one does not respond in an approved way. It is these criteria that set us up for depressive failures in life. Depression of this kind is characterized by a feeling that in some unexplainable way one has somehow failed. One may not be able to point to a particular action that should have been taken but the feeling is that one has failed simply because of what one is, i.e., "I'm just built wrong."

The fatigue that accompanies this kind of depression is genuine. It results from a 24-hour-a-day effort to ward off a collapse of self-esteem. Thoughts are shoved aside, held down, or denied and emotions are stifled, rationalized and diverted if they do not measure up to the old childhood notion of what one ought to be.

There remains just one more important question to ask in this matter. Why are we so much more easily affected by this kind of depression on some occasions than we are on others? As I have said, sometimes when we are frustrated in little ways, ways which have great personal meaning for us, we regress and in part we see the world with the eyes of a child. The same thing happens in depression that is characterized by a feeling of failure and fatigue, only in this instance we regress back to old ideals and simple but stern standards in the hope that they may become the means by which we can once again feel loved. Rather than swallowing up a loved but rejecting person, we try to swallow the bitter pill of stern, unloving morality in the hope of being loved. But regression of this kind never works and we end up feeling all the helplessness and neediness of a child and none of the support and comfort of childhood.

Thus, in both instances there is a sequence of expectation, symbolically significant disappointment, and then either an incorporation of the "loving" person who has hurt us so that the hurting person is now felt to be part of ourselves, or there is a retreat back to a frame of reference in which compliance with the rules of childhood seems to offer us the hope of achieving the loving approval of which adult life seems to have deprived us. Unfortunately the rules of childhood still do not speak to what we really are but what we "should be." And so we are once again filled with failure. For as adults we are no more able to be loving when in fact we are hurt and lonely, no more able to be charitable, when in fact we feel selfish, than we were as children. We can only engage in an exhausting attempt to be what we can never be and that spells imitation, self-hate and depression.

III

The Emotional Hazards of Your Vacation

Why are so many vacations spoiled by tension, anxiety, family feuds, and exhausting activity? They are marred by these things because we intuitively suspect that our vacations can be a dangerous time emotionally. Hence we become guarded and we divert our attention away from the freedom that frightens us with petty arguments and worries. Beneath our plans for a good time, we anticipate trouble, and so our preparations must serve a dual purpose. We not only plan in order to facilitate and enhance our opportunity for enjoyment, we also hedge on them in order to guard against the depression which many of us have unknowingly come to expect at vacation time.

Operation Over-Plan

There are two major ways to make vacation planning serve this dual function. One, the most popular in my experience, might be called "Operation Over-plan." I once had a friend who planned his vacations a year in advance. There might have been some rationale in this long-range approach if he had been married and had three or four children to be concerned about. Or his forty-eight weeks of planning might have made sense had he suffered from a financial deficit or had he been short of time. In fact, however, he was a bachelor who made more than enough money to support himself comfortably, and he was allowed to take four full weeks of vacation at almost any time of the year he chose. Besides all of this, he was a camper, and so there was very little need to spend much money, no reservations to make, and no timetable to keep. Nevertheless, he planned extensively, compulsively and almost ritualistically. Even though the detailed care he took in planning out every hour of every day sometimes approached the absurd, he never gave up. Even when other people, myself included, took his plans as a hilarious joke, he went right on. He was one of the very few people I have ever known who could seduce a fellow camper into a perfectly meaningless argument on the question of wooden vs. metal tent stakes. It goes without saying that more complicated types of equipment brought on even more elaborate arguments; arguments which were never resolved.

Of course, his planning included dry runs and weekend shakedown cruises. Not only did the tent have to be inspected for mildew, it had to be put up and taken down several times until his technique had been perfected and his best time for the procedure had been reestablished and checked with a stop watch. The hunting knife had to be honed, although he never used it, and cleaning and rearranging the already spotless tackle box was a ritual must. Last but not least, the car had to be taken through the AAA diagnostic clinic with flying colors. The arrangements were a full year-long project.

There was a time when I thought that all his efforts were a pleasure to him. I took for granted that planning for camping trips was his hobby and he enjoyed it. Then one day I saw the whole matter differently. Unexpected work at his office forced him to cancel one of the important trial trips on which he planned to check out the new citizen's band radio he had just installed in his camper. I expected him to be a little disappointed. But when I saw him that Sunday afternoon he was utterly disconsolate. None of my efforts to cheer him up helped in the least. If anything, I made the situation worse because in my friend's eyes, I was utterly unable to comprehend the seriousness of the matter.

Listening to him that Sunday afternoon was like reading a primer on psychoanalysis. He began reasonably enough. He simply lamented the fact that he had to spend the first warm, clear weekend of spring in his office rather than in the woods. But then he went on to talk about his bad luck and how he was always cheated out of the good things in life. The conversation was obviously moving toward an emotional climax that was all out of proportion to the event. For some reason the whole thing struck me as humorous. I laughed, and that did it. The poor man launched into a veritable tirade of emotion and explanation. He gave me to understand that he was completely undone and what was more important, he wanted me to understand that this kind of thing had happened to him since he was a kid. He didn't begin to wind down until he had angrily accused me of not appreciating just how important "these things" were to him; I was just like his mother who never understood a man's world. The whole sad encounter ended with a return to relative emotional normalcy and an apology from him for having lost his temper. We parted, realizing that something strange had happened which neither of us fully comprehended. It is my recollection that he carefully filed this incident away in some corner of his mind labeled "unwarranted emotional outbursts to be avoided in the future." But I was a first year resident in psychiatry, so I couldn't just file it away. I was at that stage of development when one must try out one's knowledge on any and all occasions.

It was his accusation that I had treated him like his mother that galvanized my attention. In retrospect, I realized that I was a little angry with him but at the time I denied my annoyance with an overemphasis on my intellectual understanding of his problem. It struck me that my friend's passion for camping was in complete contrast to the rest of his life. When he wasn't camping, he lived out the life of a conservative businessman except that he never talked business. He always talked about getting out into the woods, of being free, etc. Suddenly, all the Freudian symbolism fell into place for me. Correctly, but somewhat sophomorically, I realized that my friend lived his entire life trying to get away from the business life which imprisoned him. His whole life was a replay of his schoolboy's feeling of incarceration in the classroom, his impatience for vacation time, and his unspoken anger with the authority most responsible for his fate.

No wonder he was so mad when his weekend plans were interrupted. At heart he felt like a naughty schoolboy who had been planning to play hooky and now he had been caught. His weekend trial run was not a time for fun or relaxation. It was to have been a dry run for a great escape. Having to stay at the office was to him like having been caught "up to no good." He wasn't disappointed, he was ashamed, embarrassed and angry. Now I understood why he had to plan so much. He had to make his vacation look like a field exercise, an educational event, when, in fact, it was a time of truancy. And, last but not least, no wonder his friends were always uncomfortable around him. There was no fun in his planning or his trips, for at heart he was an angry boy chomping at the bit to get out of school, to be free, to leave us all behind.

I Want to Be Free

But of course, my friend was completely unaware of what he was doing. He had a rationalization for every move he made. In fact, however, his insistent planning was a giant cover up of his true feelings, i.e. his angry desire to be free. His plans were also a perfectly reasonable response to his underlying conviction that vacationing was a forbidden escape. And, of course, since his constant picking and fussing eventually aggravated everybody around him, the whole operation was a subtle expression of the frustration and conflict he felt within himself.

Since he was unaware of the basic assumptions and emotions upon which his vacation planning was predicated, he went right on with them, weekend after weekend, year after year. When his friends who were occasionally drawn into his plans, ended up disgusted if not enraged, he would then turn to me and despairingly ask, "What's wrong with people? You just can't count on them for anything." Or, "What are they upset about? All I did was try to show them a good time." While the people who had accepted his invitation to hike a trail or float a river ended up asking, "What's wrong with me? After all, he's basically a nice guy. Why does he get to me so?" They had no idea that their angry reaction was an appropriate response to my friend's disguised expression of his lifelong simmering rage at being "held down." The end result for all parties concerned was disappointment in themselves which drove them to greater efforts to make things work out. Since their greater efforts were forced and unnatural, they were denied what little hope of enjoyment remained. This led to an even greater sense of failure for my friends. Eventually everyone concerned became involved in a depressing downward spiral.

Many people actually react to their vacations as dramatically and as depressingly as my friend but it is my impression that a very large percentage of the population labors with the problem in a less dramatic form. I do not believe, however, that vacations in themselves are the problem. The problem is that vacations take us away from our daily work and that means that our basic assumptions about work are challenged. It is a known fact that very few people ever come to terms with their life's work. Seldom is work accepted as a fact of life to be contended with, mastered and finally enjoyed. Previous generations may have appeared to have solved the problem with "the work ethic" but in my experience the work ethic is all work, very little ethic, and no pleasure. It is true that people used to take pleasure in a "job well done" but I remain unconvinced that there was anything intrinsically enjoyable about the ten- to twelve-hour work day and six-day work week. There was nothing good about a paltry paycheck grudgingly given for hard work performed under miserable if not dangerous conditions. People may have been better at enduring work in the past, but I don't believe they accepted it any better. If they had, there would have been very little reason for the labor movements of the twentieth century.

It Shouldn't Be This Good

Somewhere in almost everybody's mind there is a literal belief in the Garden of Eden explanation of work, i.e. because you have eaten of the tree, "in the sweat of your face, you shall eat bread 'til you return to the ground." To some degree, most people take their work as a chore, a necessary evil which ought to be easier. Out of this belief the present generation seems dedicated to changing their work whenever they grow tired of it. Young people often express the notion that their generation has outgrown the work ethic, but it is my observation that they have simply changed the means by which they cope with the ageless conviction that labor is incarceration, a prison from which to flee. There are exceptions to this. I'm sure that to some extent, most people accept their work as a good and essential part of their lives, but in my experience even the most ardent advocates of work, the people who seem to thoroughly enjoy their work, harbor a secret desire to chuck it all.

Given these facts, it is easy to see why vacations are so often fraught with anxiety of one form or another. To many people, vacations are unconsciously viewed as a desperate bid for freedom from the world of routine labor which they cannot accept any more than an inmate can accept prison. Perhaps this seems overstated to the reader, but in fact, I believe that it is an understatement. Vacations are not only an escape from labor for most people, but they are an escape from labor which they vaguely feel they ought to suffer with. Privately, most of us feel that we once knew the pleasures of the Garden of Eden (and, of course we did in infancy) and that we lost them because we either did something wrong or something wrong was done to us. Somewhere in everybody's mind there is a small world of irrational thought; a world in which we believe that work is a deserved curse or the unavoidable result of a mistake. *We plan escapes but we are torn with guilt. Our guilt holds us back and then we hate ourselves for yielding to oppression. The more we hate ourselves, the more we throw ourselves into our work. And the more we work, the more we want to escape. So on and on the cycle goes until for some few people, vacations become an agony of planning, and for most people vacation fun is dampened down.*

I have described vacation planning that is motivated by unhealthy guilt and anger in detail. Now let me describe the second most popular way of handling the conflicts aroused by vacations. Let's take a look at the family who says, "Let's just throw everything in the car and take off for parts unknown." On the face of things, this philosophy sounds marvelously carefree and fun. And sometimes, for some people, it really is this way. I once knew a family that took a long winter weekend vacation this way. They just jumped in the car and took off. Since they had no reservations at the ski resort at which they eventually arrived, they ended up sleeping on the couches in the lobby of the lodge. That wasn't so bad. As a matter of fact it was even fun. Unfortunately, however, they had to park their car (a convertible) on a side road about a mile from the resort. When they decided to "jump in and go home" they found that the car was buried under six feet of snow. Armed with shovels, they began digging at the huge snowdrift. They started at the top and worked down. This too was fun; so much fun that someone forgot to slow down as the convertible top was approached. And so the inevitable happened. They dug right through the top of the car. The fabric ripped and someone fell in and then the snowbank gave way and half a ton of snow inundated the inside of the car. Amidst squeals of laughter, they decided on a new approach. They decided to clear the road in front of and behind the car. As a result, in forty-five minutes they were free and on their way home. The torn roof flapped away while the kids threw chunks of snow into the mountain breeze.

Scapegoating

They enjoyed the whole thing, every minute of it. I really believe they loved it but then they were an unusual family. Their fun was not dampened by sleeping on couches, the torn roof (which incidentally took piggy bank savings to repair) or the wet and cold ride from Colorado to Kansas. They enjoyed it because they were not unconsciously looking for something to relieve them of the guilt of escaping. *Had these things happened to most people, there would have been a half dozen family explosions aimed at finding a scapegoat who could carry the guilt everyone felt over their carefree abandonment of responsibility.* Many people would have unconsciously taken the untoward incidents as punishment for having dared to take time off in the first place.

Most families who "refuse" to plan are simply denying their feeling that their everyday life is something from which to escape. This system is the converse of compulsive planning but for some people it serves an identical purpose and it works much better than planning. Spontaneity that acts as a cover-up for guilt and anxiety that so often accompanies deliberate fun can easily be differentiated from spontaneity that is unencumbered by these underlying feelings. In the former case either no one has any enjoyment, or somebody has all the fun while someone else pays for it. In the latter case, people enjoy themselves and freely accept the passing inconveniences that spontaneity always brings. They are free of self-reproach and accusations.

Most "Let's jump in and go" families run into trouble about twenty-five to fifty miles out of town. (If you can get through the first two hundred miles your chances for success increase at least fifty percent and if you get through the first five hundred miles without major troubles, you have it made.) The trouble starts as soon as mom or dad or one of the kids realizes that they are too far from home to go back. Then questions that begin with, "You did remember to bring such and such, didn't you?" or, "Did you forget the so and so?" start flying. It doesn't really matter what it is that someone has forgotten. It always turns out to be an item that is absolutely essential to someone else's happiness. The first part of the underlying message that these questions convey varies from person to person. The message from mother is, "I feel bad because I didn't get the house cleaned up"; from Junior, "I feel bad because I didn't get my schoolwork done." And from dad the message is, "I feel bad because I left the office in a mess." The second part of the message, however, is the same no matter who is complaining; that is, "I wouldn't feel bad if only you hadn't forgotten the dog's flea powder, or the aspirin, or the keys to the house, or my Raggedy Ann doll." Actually the real situation is that everybody's a little unsure about being on vacation but they can all deny it by a few, "You mean to tell me you forgot . . . " type questions.

The situation can get pretty serious. I once knew a family that began to draw the battle lines when they were only a few minutes away from home. You may wonder why they didn't just turn around, pick up the forgotten items and start over again. They didn't because they were nine thousand feet in the air in a private plane. Things cooled down fast, however, when it occurred to everybody that if dear old dad, the pilot, got too upset, he just might not get them safely back to earth. By the time they touched down on the little grass runway of their resort, they were all pretty calm. But the underlying problem was still there and so things broke open again shortly after breakfast the next day.

Perhaps the problem I am talking about can best be explained by comparing two families who took identical vacations and encountered very similar troubles but who had completely different reactions. Both families lived in Chicago and they both planned to visit the northern part of the Rocky Mountain chain. Somewhere on the prairies of South Dakota, both families encountered car trouble. One family broke an oil line. Fortunately, the driver discovered the trouble before the car had lost all of its oil. The engine wasn't damaged but the local garage didn't have an oil line in stock, so they had to send twenty miles away for the part. That meant at least a half day wait for the family.

Unhappily, almost pathetically, an argument developed between the mechanic and father/husband of the family. Even though the mechanic's fee and time for installation were reasonable, he was not too subtly accused of highway robbery. The garage man held his peace and that brought the family's wife and mother to his defense. This move infuriated the husband and father and thus began an entire morning of bickering and argument. The other family was driving an old Chevy panel truck. They had a blow-out. Fortunately, no one was hurt or even shaken up but unfortunately the local gas station didn't have the special equipment needed to change truck tires and the spare was too thin to take a chance on. They too, had to wait, but there was no argument. Within minutes, one of the kids had discovered fossils in the rocks that had been dug up around the foundation of a new section of the garage. And after that discovery was enjoyed, they spent an hour and a half looking at the little town's museum of Indian and pioneer relics. By this time, it was time for lunch and then the old truck was ready and they were off.

It's the Meaning of a Vacation that Counts

The dramatic difference between the way these two families handled their delays had everything to do with the meaning their vacations had for them. It was the difference between taking a vacation that in fact was felt to be an escape from labor which they at heart felt they had no right to escape, and taking a vacation that was not an escape but a natural part of life. The first family was under such internal pressure, they couldn't possibly have weathered frustration. The second family, however, turned a frustrating delay into an enjoyable stopover simply because they were not running away from their workaday lives. They were not guilty; they were not waiting to be caught.

The words "waiting to be caught" seem to me to characterize the attitude of many people toward most of the events of their lives. I believe that this is an attitude peculiar to our society; an attitude that has grown out of our experiences of the last hundred years. During this time we have been so busy tearing down the walls of guilt and shame, prejudice and authoritarianism, that we seem to have overlooked the fact that these walls (even though they were often confining, foolish, and hurtful) had given us a psychological shelter for hundreds of years. By virtue of the walls that confined us, we used to know who we were and where we were. There were definite social, racial, economic and religious barriers beyond which the lives of most people could not extend. If the boundaries were crossed, we still knew who we were and where we were; we were pioneers in the frontier. Now, however, the boundaries are gone or are going. We are close to the point where we may reasonably consider ourselves to be citizens of the world. As a matter of fact, we may soon be at the point where it will be essential to consider ourselves in this frame of reference if we are to avoid a war that will indeed be a war to end all wars, simply because there won't be any people left to fight another one.

Don't Burn Down the House to Be Free

The freedom we now have is undeniably good but its psychological effect must be understood if we are to live successfully with it. It is unquestionably beneficial to all of us to destroy the walls that once unnecessarily confined us, but it must be remembered that not all walls are confining. Some give shelter, coherence and stability to life. To carry the analogy a little farther, it is important that one, in order to express freedom and unrestricted learning, distinguish between walking out a door of one's house and burning down one's house. Foolish as it may seem, many people seem to feel that in order to be free they should burn down their psychological house. They feel that if they don't they are asking for incarceration, i.e. copping out on freedom. In truth, however, when they have shattered all of the old taboos and crossed all of the old barriers they find themselves unable to define their existence in terms of who they are or where they are. They only know what they are not, and where they are not going back to. Like the tide, they ebb and flow in an invisible sea of loneliness.

Contrary to the appearance of certainty and confidence put up by many people these days, most of them feel a great yearning to go home again; to once again be somebody some place. But in truth they do not trust themselves enough to go back. They fear that their anxiety and loneliness may ensnare them and they will find themselves once again trapped in the old restricting ways. Many of us are like children who have run away from a bad home. We are sick and tired of living off the land, but at the same time we cannot forget the blind authority, the needless prejudice, fear and guilt that once cruelly restricted us. Nevertheless, we yearn for a place called home and we cannot be done with it. It is the yearning and wishing to know once again the comforting certainty of the past that keeps us looking for escapes. We are driven to prove and overextend our freedom in a destructive way because we are so uncomfortable with the restrictions we associate with rest. And since vacations are a prime opportunity to be "free" we perceive them as the great challenge of our year.

The pace of life in our time has little to do with the excitement of real freedom. It has everything to do with our ceaseless need to deny our lonely isolation. Just beneath the surface, we hope to be found. We yearn to be brought back. We are waiting to be caught.

Perhaps this is the way things must be for a while, but let us hope that a few of us will soon discover that we need not be children all of our lives. Independent, capable adults can be free and they can also go "home," and as such they need not fear incarceration. Going home, reestablishing some of our traditions, reexamining some of our former ideals, and readopting some of the old rules need not be a capitulation to all the needless limits of the past. On the contrary, a careful reexamination of our past and a free acceptance of the good parts of it may just save us from our desire to be caught. And it is important that we be saved from this. For once we are caught and forced back, we will indeed find ourselves incarcerated. There will be no freedom to choose; no freedom to accept or reject.

In this chapter, I have used vacations as a symbol of the depressing "escape psychology" that permeates our lives. It is depressing because we find ourselves so busy being free that we have no freedom. Again, we are dealing with a psychological spiral. This time it is a spiral in which the harder we try to achieve freedom, the less freedom we can allow ourselves. Finally we run out of energy and we regress and become helpless, frightened infants who are no longer free to choose wise limits. We become wards of our own foolishness.

What can we do about it? Of course, "we can slow down," "take it easy," and "place reasonable limits on ourselves." However, given the momentum of our society, these well-intended admonitions are not likely to be heard, or if heard, they are not likely to have more than a temporary, superficial effect. In the long run, they may ever spur us on toward more frantic activity. If we are to help ourselves, we must dare to recognize the core of fear and loneliness in us all. *We must dare to see that much of what we call "getting away from it all" is in fact an isolating effort to separate ourselves from our past and our work.* It is an effort that can become every bit as restricting as was the past from which we run. It is not enough to have escaped. To be free we must reexamine the walls of yesterday's "prison" and out of them build a home for today. Then our frantic, depressing efforts to escape can cease. Then there can be freedom.

How can we help ourselves? We can understand that vacations are usually overloaded with emotional expectations. Throughout the long winter months our reasonable, happy expectations are gradually intensified because they come to stand for relief from all that is difficult in life. In our hearts we know that no vacation can give us all that we want. So why not climb down off the pinnacle of unreal expectations before we pack the first bag? Why not back down to a place where we can see just how laughably unreal our hopes were?

Peak experiences are good. They are to be sought after but by the same token they must be allowed to slip away if we are to regain our freedom. The secret in this process lies in knowing that this slipping away is not a defeat. It is an advance toward freedom and the creative recreation that evolves from freedom.

IV

Recreation:
Let It Happen

If vacations, when viewed as an escape from work inevitably lead us to a disappointing letdown if not a depressing sense of isolation, then what alternatives do we have? One obvious alternative is not to escape from it, but to take it right along with us. Usually this goes under the heading of "combining business with pleasure." What about the business vacation? Sometimes some people can make the combination work for them, but more often than not, their underlying motivation for this approach (their desire to avoid the escape psychology that has let them down before) spoils the hoped for fun. From a psychological standpoint, there is only one thing more pathetically self-defeating than a family racing down the superhighway with ten thousand dollars worth of auto and trailer equipment in a mad attempt to "make five hundred miles today," and that is the working vacation, i.e. two weeks of business meetings, sales lectures, and convention parties with side trips to the zoo, botanical gardens and golf for "the ladies" thrown in.

The only possible conscious rationale for this potpourri of business and pleasure stems from the Internal Revenue Service rules on business deductions. The underlying idea is to get something for nothing, to make the "vacation" a bargain, a good deal. There is no question that many people can indeed save a few dollars this way, but I have never quite been able to understand why people want to save money in such a way that they spoil the thing they are buying. A number of years ago an auto manufacturer discovered that the price of an automobile could be substantially reduced if the vehicle were redesigned to have two wheels in the back and just one in the front. Many of these vehicles were sold and the people who bought them did indeed save money. But it is also true that the frugal owners of these three-wheeled vehicles were stuck with a machine that was so unstable that it could not turn a corner at fifteen miles an hour.

Most of the time business vacations are the product of this kind of psychological serendipity. One may indeed save a little money and have a little fun, but the entire project is based on such unstable psychological ground that it is very likely to be remembered as a fortunate achievement rather than a vacation. Having said this, I have again implied that vacations are very special to me. A vacation is not just anything that takes us away from work nor is it sightseeing at a savings. Since both of these approaches to vacations are psychologically negative in nature, they run contrary to the real purpose of vacations, i.e. recreation. Recreation means to recreate, to bring alive again. Recreation is a creative process, and it cannot be forced, but by the same token it does not just happen because we have gotten away from something or because we have gotten away with something.

"Total" Relaxation Is Hard Work

Up to this point, most of my criticism has dealt with vacations that are just too much. They are overdone. But there is another popular approach which appears to be the exact psychological opposite of the too-much vacation. Perhaps we could call it the "too-little" vacation. In this case, one makes work out of not working. Psychologically skimpy vacations usually fall under the "All I want to do is relax" category. The underlying assumption seems to be that our daily life has us all wound up and vacation should be a chance to unwind. Of course, there is an element of rational thinking to this philosophy but supporters of the viewpoint are often possessed by fantasies that are in sharp contrast to their underlying desires. "All I want to do is sit on the beach and watch the waves and feel the wind," is a reasonable enough fantasy. However, when these reasonable, relaxed seekers of quietude end up screaming at their kids for making a few innocuous waves of their own, one must suspect that their announced rationale disguises some very strong unstated desires.

A desire to free one's mind of the pressure of the workaday world is a perfectly reasonable and healthy desire, but some people kid themselves with this kind of talk. What they desperately desire is Nirvana and so they work at it. They make a project of a search for the vacant mindedness of infancy. In itself there is still nothing very unhealthy about this idea, but in fact very few people can stand to achieve it. Two weeks alone in August on the side of a mountain is neither the time nor the place to attempt to achieve the serenity of an Indian Yogi who has practiced his art daily for half a century.

Nirvana Can Be Frightening

"Nature abhors a vacuum," is an aphorism particularly true for psychological inactivity. People who try too hard to empty their minds too often find themselves successful beyond their wildest dreams. The emptiness they find is anything but peace-producing. It turns out that the daily routine that so often seems oppressive to us is in fact a means by which we keep ourselves comfortably preoccupied so that we will not have to face our underlying lack of substance. How many times have you heard a disgruntled vacationer say, "I just get settled and then so-and-so happens"? Of course, there are genuine interruptions to one's solitude. Babies do cry at mealtimes, the mosquitoes do indeed come out around sunset and sometimes people in the next campsite do play their portable radio at an unconscionable volume. But many times people who claim to want to settle down begin to reach for and find things to disturb them.

The mother who can't stand more than five minutes of solitude without "checking on the kids" is probably not just a conscientious mother. She is probably so accustomed to being harried that when she has a chance to let down she finds herself unbearably anxious. She approaches contemplation like a tourist riding a donkey down one of the steep trails into the Grand Canyon. It's beautiful, it's gorgeous, it's fantastic, but something inside the rider keeps saying, "Whoa." Of course the trailmaster tells the rider that the donkey has been down the trail so many times that he could do it blindfolded. "It's all been done by thousands of other people." But of course that doesn't help very much because the rider isn't really worried about the donkey or thousands of other people. The rider is worried about himself and somewhere out of his primitive urge for self-preservation he knows that it will be too late to say "Whoa" after the animal has decided to break with tradition and try the short way down, i.e. right over the cliff.

Canyons of Thought and Panic

"Right over the cliff" pretty well describes the near panic some people feel when they decide to try for "complete relaxation."

Complete relaxation can mean a leap into a canyon of thought and feeling which, while beautiful to observe from afar, is terrifying to really descend into. With time to think, time to give some real thought to the meaning and purpose of one's life, many people find that they have simply taken for granted that they have something to think about. They may find, however, that all they really have are bits and pieces of childhood philosophy, scraps of folklore, unexamined religious convictions and a few goals for life that haven't been reviewed for twenty years. On the face of it, this condition simply suggests that they have a lot of thinking to do. That is true, but to their terror they find that unless one has a few reliable, well thought out ideas upon which to ride, one may be left with the feeling that one's thoughts are like the planets of the universe, i.e. masses of sterile rock ever increasing the measureless distance that lies between them.

Usually people who embark on this trail of terror can check their condition by simply drumming up a few distractions. Worries, chores, endless little charities for the happiness of others, arguments, and booze can usually save the day. Notice, however, that once again the vacationer is busy escaping, only this time he is escaping from himself.

Occasionally people caught up in the fear of vacancy don't, or can't, find outside distractions. Then inside distractions have to be found. Have you ever lain on your belly in the sand of a quiet beach expecting to "really think things through," only to find yourself preoccupied with the thump of your heartbeat on the warm sand beneath you? At first it's an innocuous or slightly irritating interruption to your thoughts and so you turn over on your back only to discover for the first time in your life that when you look up into the clear blue sky your field of vision is cluttered with little translucent, hairlike particles that keep floating around the inside of your eyes. (This is a harmless condition common to middle-aged people. It rarely gets worse, seldom improves, and is nothing to worry about.) If this discovery doesn't distract your attention, you'll more than likely have to worry about some other unimportant physical manifestation or life, i.e. the rolling of your stomach, your breathing, or last but not least, the stinging sunburn you've gotten while all of this is going on.

Actually these distractions are a small price to pay for the relief from the anxiety that arises when people who spend their lives without much reflection suddenly decide to take a vacation trip into the land of thought. I once had a patient who couldn't distract himself, call me from a forest ranger's fire tower just to get a little reassurance that the absolute emptiness he'd found in himself while hiking the Appalachian Trail alone could be filled in. Happily I knew the man well enough to be able to honestly reassure him and so he finished the trip, but not without a few sleepless nights under the stars.

Voices Out of Emptiness

The only thing more frightening than silent mindlessness is an explosion of thoughts, ideas and feelings that are utterly foreign to one's ordinary image of oneself. In fact, this is the condition which empty-headedness tries to avoid. In other words, when I reassured my patient that the painful void with which he was suffering could be overcome, I was not quite candid with him. I knew that his condition would eventually give way to a barrage of thoughts, feelings and memories that would be extremely painful to him. I withheld this insight because I did not want him to be alone when the mental silence he abhorred was broken by voices he would find terrifying.

Unfortunately, many people do not have anyone to turn to when emptiness brought on by an overdone attempt to "be alone and think" gives way to more thoughts than one can comprehend. Their reaction is shock, dismay, and guilt. People suddenly deprived of the ordinary external distractions of life, (such as vacationers bent on being alone), may end up depressed and demoralized when they are forced to own up to themselves. Of course finding out the truth about oneself is good but there is a time and a place for it. The truth is good to know only if it can be understood and most of the time understanding does not come in a burst of insight while one is dramatically perched on a pile of seashore rocks. Most of the time, the goodness of truth comes slowly as we learn to face facts within the context of a lasting, reliable, loving relationship. Truth that is inadvertantly forced on one usually arouses so much anxiety that its healing, enriching effect is lost.

Having criticized vacations in which one tries to "escape" by doing too much as well as vacations in which one tries to "escape" by doing too little, the reader might conclude that I am simply pointing the way toward a dull, "happy" medium. Nothing could be further from the truth. It is true, and I mention this as a side issue, that we would all do well to try to match our vacations to our needs, keeping in mind that thinking in solitude is heavy work, and unless one is used to it, it should be done cautiously. But the real point I'd like to make is that vacations are supposed to be creative and creativity has nothing to do with either strained or effortless escapes. Creativity as it is found in the unusually talented person is an enormously complex subject which need not concern us here. I am simply talking about the ordinary kind of creativity which enables the vacationer to end a day of sightseeing, or gardening, or reading and meditation, or travel or just meeting with old friends with the feeling that he or she has been changed and enriched by the day's experiences.

De-escalation

For most people the greatest hindrance to this kind of creativity is their ingrained need to feel that they have "done" something. We seem to feel that we must do something about everything. We have so completely usurped the role of nature in our lives that we have lost faith in it. We cannot leave anything alone. If we decide to take a trip, we must prove that we can take five hundred miles of driving in stride. There can be no side trips, no spontaneous stopovers, no "wasted days." If we encounter a detour we are obliged to feel irritated, even though it may take us through a half dozen beautiful little towns which we would otherwise have missed. If we decide to meditate, we must plunge into a frightening solitude even though our instincts tell us that the depths we reach for may be too much for us to stand. If we visit friends, it must become a party. Creativity does require effort but the question is what kind of effort does it take? *Most vacationers are quite unaware that the most important effort they can put forth is an effort to sensibly reduce their efforts.* In this respect the first forty-eight hours of a vacation are crucial. During these first two days, one can either put forth an effective effort to de-escalate one's life, or one will defeat the recreational aspect of the remainder of the vacation by trying harder and harder in one way or another to get the most out of everything.

De-escalation is a critically important concept to understand if one's vacation is to have any recreational value whatsoever. Obviously it is not accomplished when we simply exchange one kind of mad dash for another. And just as obviously it is not a matter of sinking into a frightening oblivion. De-escalation simply means searching for a private environment; a personal frame of reference in which aspects of oneself which are ordinarily hidden, may emerge. It is a matter of discovering that one has the capacity to respond to oneself, to others and to situations in ways that are qualitatively different and new.

Let me explain it this way. Creativity so far as vacations go, is like being a good farmer. If one wants to grow a vegetable garden, there is some essential effort to be made. But there is also a time to wait. Most vacations are conducted in a way analogous to the farming of a city dweller recently turned fanatical agriculturalist. He assumes that since corn grows better when it is cultivated and fertilized, it will grow even better if it is dug up every day and drowned in manure. He cannot conceptualize himself as an assistant to nature who must spend a great deal of time waiting for things to develop. He cannot accept the idea that there are natural limits which must be observed, limits which, if exceeded, will destroy growth.

The analogy holds good in another way. A farmer must take risks. He must accept the fact that even when he has done his best to plant and cultivate there is no guarantee of a good harvest. The same is true of vacations. One must be willing to risk them and since we count on them so much, this is an extremely hard thing to do. Of course, I'm not talking about leaving hotel reservations to chance and car maintenance to sheer luck. I am referring to personal risk, the risk involved in letting things occur rather than making them happen.

But what about eagerness, enthusiasm, and excitement? Are we supposed to let all of that go in favor of a bovine passivity? On the contrary, the process I am describing is a process in which one discovers excitement and stimulation. The point is, however, that enthusiasm that is recreational rather than a drummed-up, exhausting experience comes from inside of ourselves. It emerges because we are willing to stand aside from ourselves and risk failure in the hope that refreshing psychological change will replace the sterile "snapshot" loneliness that always follows artificial activities that separate ourselves from ourselves. It is a matter of internal discovery rather than external, forced activity.

Years ago my family and I spent ten days camping out in the mountains of northwest Montana. We had hardly settled in when the entire camping area was blasted by the roar of a couple of highpowered motorcycles. I was furious. I was quick to assume (and it turned out that I was right) that the two couples, a boy and a girl on each bike, were immoral, drug-using hippies. Remembering, however, that as a psychoanalyst I should be able to accept people and to understand them, I sat down and started to work. In other words, I wasn't fifteen hundred miles away from my office. I had just set up practice in the middle of a Rocky Mountain pine forest. Fortunately, the whole effort quickly failed. I really didn't want to understand these people. I was tired of understanding people and so I just went ahead and got mad. But that didn't last long either. Gradually it dawned on me that the noise that had set me off had ceased. The only sound coming from the cyclists' campsite was the sound of guitar music and folk songs. I tried to keep my square-headed, conservationist, anti-pollutionist, righteous anger going. But I couldn't because eventually I realized that the only thing that was really bothering me was that empty, slightly frightening feeling common to all vacationers who have finally arrived at their destination after a frantic trip on the freeways. I knew then that what really bothered me was me. I was afraid to let down, but I did and when I did I found myself ready for discovery.

The next morning I paid the cyclists a visit and in twenty minutes I discovered that all my life I had wanted to ride a motorcycle and, what is more important, I discovered that hippie-type young people can be loving and enjoyable when one dares to talk, to listen and perhaps even to let an idea or two take root.

And contrary to my shortsighted convictions about myself, I discovered that I could enjoy talking and listening to them. The cyclists were still there when we left but a day later they passed us on the highway. We recognized each other instantly. We honked and they waved. It was only ten seconds of recognition but it was ten seconds that changed the nature of our entire vacation because in that ten seconds I knew that I was somebody who could change; I was different and I loved it. Somewhere in the country are four hippies that I love very much because they helped me discover that I have the capacity to enjoy people whose way of life is antithetical to my own and because that discovery saved a "well planned vacation" from depression; it turned around into a gently creative experience.

There is grave danger that the reader will interpret what I have said as implied advice or even as an admonition. Actually I wish I could put things in this frame of reference. It's a well known fact that writers of psychological material who tell people what to do and how to do it are enormously popular. Unfortunately, they are authors who are popular because they appeal to our childish hope that an easy way can be found to deal with everything. We all want to "tidy things up," "have it all knocked out," or "be on top of things." But notice that every time we succumb to the urge to squeeze life into these narrow frames of reference we are obliged either to look to the success of other people for proof that it can be done, or we must distance ourselves from the facts of our own lives.

We are more likely to look to others for validation of the idea that "life can be beautiful," because it is easier to focus on their successes. (Their failures are always carefully hidden.) If we are to use ourselves as the prototype of the "on top of things" life, we must work hard to remain unaware of our shortcomings. But it is human nature to think that somewhere somebody "has it made." It's an easy assumption to make, particularly since there are so many people around us who are willing to win fame and fortune by supporting our very human desire to continue the illusion that life can be "managed." We all know that the person who really believes that he is "a self-made man" is a deluded fool, but somehow we can't help but believe that it might be true and that it must be great to be that way.

In our hearts, we know that the so-called secure life is an illusion. We know that it is an illusion that estranges us from the true facts of life and from ourselves. We may even realize that when estrangement happens, we have lost everything worthwhile in life and there really isn't anything left to make secure. Yet every time a vacation comes along, we are tempted to try to make it work. This time the car isn't going to act up. We have really gotten all of the bugs out of it. And this time we're really going to do things in an organized way. But then the very means we have invented to make things go right begin to stultify our creativity.

Everything that makes a vacation recreational, and for that matter, everything that makes life really worth living, must take an inferior priority. Somehow we know all of this but we go right on. The means may change but the effect is the same. There is very little difference between the people who put their faith in a new Cadillac and those who distort their faith in God to achieve static security. Both will let them down. The only difference is that the Cadillac will let one down because it is going to run out of gas and God will let one down because the divine cannot be incapsulated within a bootstrap security operation. But we keep on trying. We try because it is the nature of mankind to strive to free himself of fear.

Here is the rub. No one wants to think that we are locked into fear. We want to believe that we can overcome everything.

We will listen to anyone who has a scheme or a philosophy or a theology that is a guarantee to give us "successful living," power, and freedom from fear. But unhappily we are part of God's world. We exist in a universe that cannot be remolded to match our every need. The fantastic advances of science notwithstanding, there is still much mystery in our world and sometimes the unknown is realistically frightening.

The point of all this is to say that I cannot dictate specific ways to avoid the vacation pitfalls I have talked about. And I will not presumptuously lay before you a half dozen surefire ways of making vacations truly recreational rather than exhausting and depressing. I cannot tell you these things because the things we do that keep us from newness of life are not foolish accidents that can be overcome with someone else's methods. They are purposeful "accidents" meant to spare us a recognition of the fear inherent in letting go of the daily routines and ordinary assumptions which enable us to believe that we can control life and take the fear out of it. To set ourselves apart from daily life is to realize that we are part of a much larger life; a life too large to control and that is frightening. My only concrete advice is this: judiciously try to exchange control of your petty world for participation in a world that is beyond your control. In the end, however, the deciding factor will be your willingness to be afraid, to sit still and meditate (be careful to keep it somewhat organized), to look and listen and know that you are very small. Then and only then are you ready for creation. For creation is not made, but discovered. Recreation is not manufactured, it is allowed to happen.

A few years ago my family and I took a trip with another family. One peaceful afternoon, Pete, the husband and father of the other family, and I decided to climb a twelve-thousand-foot mountain just for fun. Actually the climb was not unrealistic since our campsite was at an altitude of nine thousand feet. The mountain looked like an easy climb and the view promised to be magnificent. We arose before dawn, threw a few emergency provisions into a haversack and took off. As we ascended the mountain, it was like climbing from night into day. The valley and its lake were still dark but the sun had already touched the top of the mountain. When we crossed from darkness into light, we paused to look back at the lake and our campsite which were now emerging into the half-light of dawn.

The climb had been strenuous but thoroughly enjoyable. Now, however, we approached the summit and there were some decisions to be made; we discovered that there were more risks involved in the final phase of our ascent than we had anticipated. Since it never occurred to us to turn back, we cautiously made our way through tight passages and across narrow ledges. Finally we broke out into the open. All that lay between us and the summit were a couple of hundred yards of snow and ice. The view from the top was all that we had anticipated and more. The air was cold, clean and blowing. While we sat in the clear mountain sunshine, we watched a snowstorm thirty miles or so away. The earth looked like a miniature garden; we felt like gods.

After lunch, we began planning our descent. The plan was for us to be back in camp by mid-afternoon so that we could take care of the kids for a while and give our wives a chance for freedom. Unhappily, it soon became apparent that the trail that seemed safe enough going up the mountain did not look at all safe going down. The situation grew a little tense when we realized that we were without rope or any other climbing equipment and that we had no more than a half day's supply of food and water. After two hours of investigating every possible mode of descent, it became obvious that the only way open to us was down the smooth, grassy backside of the mountain that faded

into a maze of foothills and streams. We got down without incident, but once down we found ourselves without landmarks.
Obviously we had to circumvent the entire mountain in order to
get back to our campsite. But since mountains are ringed by
lesser mountains, each with its own gorges and ledges and loose
rocks, there was no open way back. Clearly, we were not lost.
All we had to do was to keep in view the peak we had climbed
and keep bearing to the right. Sooner or later we had to come
out where we had started. But the peak was not always visible.
Sometimes we ran into dead ends, i.e. three-hundred-foot cliffs
of granite, and sometimes we had to reverse our direction in order
to find a place to ford a torrential mountain stream.

We were not scared and certainly we were not terrified, but
we were unquestionably anxious. The anxiety bothered me. I
couldn't understand why I should be so anxious when obviously
time and labor would eventually bring us home. Then I realized
that my anxiety had nothing to do with time and labor. It had
to do with the simple fact that I had started this day full of hope
and expectations and I had been fulfilled but only for an hour,
and then I had to descend into wilderness. I was an unimportant figure in a land that silently frustrated my every effort to
feel that I was master of my fate.

As the day ground on, I became oppressively aware of a sense
of insignificance. At first I comforted myself by thinking that
if only I had bothered to bring along a little equipment things
would have gone much better. But that was short-lived comfort
for I soon recognized that no amount of equipment could have
spared me the anxiety I felt. Equipment could not have fore-
stalled my realization of relative insignificance. Every rock,
every tree and every stream was a formidable barrier. I wasn't
helpless, lost or out of control, but I was small, very, very small.

Then a quiet change in my mood began to occur. The more

I owned up to my emotions, the more I began to get the feel of the countryside. I began to be able to tell a dead-end gorge from a genuine pass. I gave up checking my position relative to the mountain because gradually I came to know where I was even though the land was just as rough and home was almost as far away. My friend was puzzled by my change in mood. I was actually happy, almost joyful. It was while I was in this mood that we reached what was for me the highpoint of the day. We found ourselves surrounded by jagged hills. They were small enough to climb safely and easily, but we had been up so many similar hills only to find that there was a one-hundred-foot cliff on the other side, that we paused to discuss which one to take a chance on. We made our decision, and moved toward the top. Once there, we found ourselves on the edge of a gorgeous mountain meadow that stretched for miles down to the edge of the lake and home. I hesitate to add the last detail of this story because it might sound contrived. As we climbed the last hill, I found myself whistling Bach's "Sheep May Safely Graze." When we reached the top of the hill, there were the sheep; a whole herd of them quietly grazing within the sight of a weathered shepherd and his dogs.

Vacations are life in miniature. The auspicious beginnings, the planning or the deliberate non-planning, the glorious ascent and the thrilling opportunity to gain an entirely new perspective on things are all there. But many times the creative part comes on the way down when plans don't work out, perspectives are lost, and when one's significance dwindles from the inflated proportions that it had attained throughout the year. The creative part happens when we are just a little lost, just enough out of control that we may rediscover that we are securely and safely a part of God's world.

What can we do about vacation depressions? I think it's time we realize that vacations are too important to be ruined by futile efforts to make our precious daydreams come true. Vacations are for real. They are a real part of life. They involve risk and discovery, frustration and fulfillment. Putting this idea to work can mean different things to different people. There is no list that I could invent that would speak to individuals with any accuracy. You must invent the particular means by which your vacation is rescued from being a "fantastic," depressing failure and made a time of recreation.

V

I Dread Christmas

Jim Williams, the middle-aged man who sat before me, stared through the window in my office at the raging blizzard outside. After long moments of silence, he began quietly to unfold the story of his depression. "I'll never forget the Christmas of '56. I had graduated from college the year before and I had a good job. This was the first time that we could spend a few dollars. The kids were old enough to enjoy a really first-rate Christmas tree so I shelled out twelve dollars and fifty cents (a lot of money in '56) for a fifteen-foot Scotch pine tree. Since it was much too big to fit into any room in the house, I decided to place it in the stairwell that went from the entrance hall to the second floor. A stand substantial enough to hold the tree would have been too expensive, and so we decided to suspend the tree from the bannister of the second floor stairwell. Everybody seemed happy. My wife got a piece of clothesline from the basement and the kids fairly flew up to the second floor and took positions on the staircase where they could watch the placement of the 'biggest tree in the world.' I tied the rope to the top of the tree and prepared to stand it up on end. The plan was for my thirteen-year-old son to catch the rope and secure it to the railing as soon as I got the tree standing upright. Getting hold of the trunk of a Scotch pine that has six-foot branches is like skinning a porcupine, but I managed. I managed, but my son didn't. As I struggled to hold the tree upright, he kept grabbing for the rope which was always a little out of his reach. It was out of his reach because I couldn't hold the tree completely steady, and because he was so convulsed by laughter and delight, (egged on by his mother and sisters), he simply couldn't control himself.

"Then a strange and terrible thing began to happen to me. As I felt myself losing my strength and ability to hold the tree upright, I found the joy and pleasure of the occasion draining out of me. Suddenly I was emotionally helpless. I laid the tree back down and then, to my own horror and pain, I flew into a rage. To my complete chagrin, I found myself swearing at my son, insulting my wife, and devastating my daughters with anger. It didn't last long but for me that was the end of Merry Christmas for 1956. The family recovered in a few hours. They even apologized for 'fooling around,' but I could not forgive myself. In some vague way I knew that my rage had nothing to do with their happy foolishness.

"We finally got the tree up that evening after a well organized, sober attempt, but for me the fun was gone from the event. I felt like I'd been bitten by a snake, like I was in the coils of a depressing force that gradually squeezed all the joy out of the entire Christmas season, the first Christmas we thought we were really free. That was fifteen years ago but I still feel sad when I remember it. At the time it seemed to me that I had ruined the whole family's Christmas, but the truth is they hardly remembered it. Just a few years ago, I asked my son if he remembered the incident. After a minute of reflection, he finally said, 'Oh, yeah. You mean the time you blew your stack, when I couldn't catch the rope. Yeah, I remember, that was really something.' And then he began to laugh all over again. My God, what's wrong with me?"

By this time my patient was in tears. Recalling the story had made him almost as sad as he was that Christmas evening in 1956. He was despondent all over again.

Our hour was over and it was our last meeting before the Christmas break. As he stood up to leave he said, "The only good thing I can say about this Christmas is that at least there's one person in my life now who isn't going to say, 'Merry Christmas' and expect to hear a happy 'Same to you' in response. At least there's one person who understands, and that's good even if I have to pay you for it."

In a sense my patient's question, "My God, what's wrong with me?" was perfectly reasonable. What possible reason was there for him to have suffered three weeks of depression over one ten-minute blow-up? Why should he have gotten depressed all over again when he recounted the story to me? It's understandable that he should have felt remorse for a while and it is also understandable that he should still remember the incident. But he was describing something far more important than just a passing bad feeling over an unfortunate incident. He was expressing depression; a nagging painful conviction that there was something basically wrong with him.

His question made even more sense when we consider the circumstances surrounding the incident. It was Christmas; a time of happiness and joy. He had some money, a secure job and a little free time to spend with his family. For years he had gone to school during the day and worked evenings. Now that was over. It's easy to understand a blow-up or a temporary loss of temper, but why did he get depressed? Why did it still bother him years later?

The Happiness Bind

To understand this question, we must remember that Christmas to many people is almost a commandment to be happy. Just as people used to fast and pray during Holy Week because it was the proper attitude to maintain during the commemoration of Christ's passion and death, most people still feel that it is "proper" to be happy during the season in which we celebrate Christ's birth. The trouble with these "proper" attitudes is that they tend to interrupt the normal ebb and flow of everyday emotions. They stifle the feelings that are natural to daily life. The super serious attitude that was once "proper" for Lent and Holy Week is almost a thing of the past. But the propriety of manipulating oneself into a merry atmosphere during Christmas has overgrown its religious dimensions and has become a modern social law. Since there is very little theological rationale for this forced joy we all feel obliged to express during the Christmas season, we are probably right in concluding that it is largely sustained for economic reasons. "Happy" people who are not free to be themselves pay well for the merchandise of pleasure. Be that as it may, we must still contend with the fact that most people feel obligated to be happy during Christmas. They are even apologetic if they slip up and break the spell. In short, we are driven to adopt an unnatural emotional stance. We are trapped. We feel guilty if we aren't happy because then, supposedly, we are letting everybody down, i.e. we're not joining in the spirit. And we are guilty if we go on acting happy if in fact we know that often our expressed emotion is overdone and sometimes downright false.

Paradoxically, Christmas, the season to be jolly, creates an atmosphere in which we are all the more susceptible to unhappiness and depressive emotions, than we are to joy. My patient's Christmas depression contained other paradoxes that are often shared by us all. He had worked long and hard to achieve his modest success and now he had a little money to spend and a little leisure time to enjoy. The paradox is that the first thing he did with his success was to spend his money on something that was much too big to handle. I'm well aware that there are times when we must let caution go and be free, even foolishly free with ourselves. There is a time to be joyfully open with ourselves and share our joy with those we love. But it is also true that much of what passes for joyful abandonment is in fact an impulsively-driven expression of trumped-up emotions which, in our society, usually ends up costing money we had no intention of spending.

Of course, it never looks this way. It didn't appear to my patient to be this way. All he seemed to want to do was to give his kids a really great Christmas tree, but in fact he spent three times as much as he wanted to spend for something that was twice as large as he wanted to handle. In one simple act he deprived himself of money, time, and the freedom to enjoy his family. Realistically, he only overspent himself by ten dollars and it only took an entire Sunday rather than just a Sunday evening to decorate the lavishly large tree. But the realistic aspects of the event were not the cause of this man's depression. Somewhere just beneath the surface of his conscious mind, he felt that he had been had. He felt he'd squandered the money, time, and freedom he had worked so hard for. His family felt lightheartedly foolish but he felt like a fool.

The other paradox of this man's Christmas, a paradox which we all share at one time or another, was his assumption that bigger and better would make for more spirit and happiness. No one in their right mind really believes that bigger purchases, bigger parties, and more extravagant ceremonies are really going to make for more joy. Every parent knows that most children can have just as much fun with a small inexpensive present or party or Christmas tree as they can with the elaborate, time-consuming affairs that must be so "deeply" appreciated and treated with such care. But the point is that the modern Christmas is not a time of right-mindedness. It is a setup, an emotional pressure cooker, an introduction to depression. *In the name of the holiday spirit we deprive ourselves of our freedom to be ourselves and then when we hate ourselves for doing it, we must feel guilty for "not getting into the spirit."* In the hope of participating in a mood of joy and good will, we drive ourselves and incarcerate our emotions in a prison named "Merry Christmas."

Of course, these factors do not completely explain the depression which my patient suffered. But they do explain why so many millions of people are made more susceptible to depression during Christmas. The unadorned facts that underlie our modern celebration of Christmas explain very well why so many people look forward to the season to be jolly with hopefulness that is tinged with apprehensiveness and unhappy memories of Christmases past.

The Christmas Setup

It is true that Christmas sets us up. We are very liable to feel guilty sometime during the season and often the guilt spirals downward toward depression. But the external circumstances of our life are rarely solely responsible for our unhappy feelings. Usually there are internal problems which are brought to the foreground by external conditions. Thus, the man we have been talking about was not only more vulnerable to depression because of the bind that Christmas put him in, but he also brought to Christmas expectations, ideas and wishes which were readily activated by the influence of the season and which then had to lead to depression. Take, for example, the fact that he was looking forward to Christmas as a golden time during which he could "let down." He had "arrived"; he could "relax." For years he had been looking forward to the security and freedom he had at last achieved. But actually security, freedom, and money did not represent an achievement of maturity. In actuality they meant the recapturing of the beautiful, simple security of childhood. In other words, for years this man had been looking forward to going backwards.

Recapturing Childhood and Disillusionment

Unfortunately, when success is conceptualized in this way, (and for most of us it is to one degree or another), disillusionment is inevitable. It is inevitable because adult success can never come close to providing the love and security of childhood. Yet this is exactly what we are urged to expect from Christmas. Magazine articles and TV programs constantly present us with a picture of Christmas as a "beautiful happening." It is a time when homes are to be decorated with all the skills of a professional artist, a time when families are supposed to be held together harmoniously by the love generated by the season, and a time when food and gifts are bountifully given and freely accepted, irrespective of the balance in the checkbook.

We are made to feel that Christmas is a supreme opportunity to become a "success." Economically limited people are driven to indebtedness that might take months to pay off in order to avoid the ultimate failure in American life, a poor Christmas. But the poor who must strive to achieve the epitome of success, i.e. a bountiful, overdone and over-indulged holiday, are less liable to become depressed than those of us who have achieved the success for which others must strive. This is true simply because the man or woman who has actually achieved the dream must face the fact that success is not satisfying; the old yearning goes right on and the old wishes press forward.

The Failure of Success

Perhaps by this time you have guessed why my patient blew up, why he was so enraged in the midst of a light-hearted occasion. He was enraged because for him it was only superficially a light-hearted occasion. Just beneath the surface of his external emotions the occasion was a deeply serious matter. He was a "success" and now things were supposed to go smoothly, tensions were supposed to relax and most important of all, there was now supposed to be free time. But his son didn't catch the rope. The tree cost too much and now there would be no time in which to be a homegrown Andy Williams. His fantasy of the successful Christmas was shot. Someone had failed to catch on and now there was no wealth, there was just a few paltry dollars that couldn't possibly sustain the propped-up beauty of a TV special. And there was no time to be free. There was just another weekend. Unconsciously, Christmas to this man and to millions like him meant a chance to step away from life. It was to be a chance to be "above it all," the way a child is comfortably above the facts of life. It was a chance to float along on clouds of expectation and hopefulness.

Deception and the Great Letdown

To the reader all of this might simply suggest that my patient was a hopeless dreamer, an immature and superficial man who just hadn't grown up. As a matter of fact, these things are true but they are true of millions of people. And so why don't we all get over it, cut it out and grow up? There are a lot of reasons why we don't do these things but the one I'd like to emphasize at this time is the fact that we rarely realize what we are doing. We can't deal with something we don't know exists and most of us just don't realize that our Christmas expectations are grounded on childish hopefulness and adolescent romanticism.

Let me hasten to remind you that I am not depreciating either childish hopefulness or romanticism. It would be a painful world indeed if people couldn't on occasion slip away from the restricting bonds of everyday reality and allow themselves to be full of expectations and hopefulness. There is nothing unhealthy about it and there needn't be any letdown. However, such occasions are acknowledged times of relief. They are times set aside to have fun, to be young again and to be carefree; they are not times of deception which must be kept going at all costs lest the bubble burst. But, somehow, during the modern Christmas season, we are driven to conclude that all the hopes and dreams of all the Christmases past can and "should" be met. We are led to believe that everything is possible and so we are set up for a letdown. But, of course, we are carefully set up so that the letdown won't come until we have exhausted our energies, time and money on ceaseless cleaning, arranging, decorating, shopping, and most exhausting of all, manipulating our entire family into a mood of sterilized, consistent happiness that militates against the joy of Christmas.

And we don't even know that we are doing it. We can't calm

down, we can't call a halt to the spiral toward deflation because we honestly believe that we are trying to have a good time. We are completely unaware that most of the underlying motives for our Christmas madness have nothing to do with a good time. In fact, we are in the grips of the reawakened, insatiable hopes of childhood and we don't know it. Christmas is not just a party, a special celebration, an anticipated evening for love by the fireplace, or a day to enjoy the kids, or a joyful religious holiday. It has become a two-and-one-half-month period of deadly serious effort to make life work the way it was "supposed to work." It is a two-and-one-half-month effort to satisfy, in one way or another, the silently aroused hopes of childhood.

Understanding Helps

There are some obvious advantages to understanding these underlying psychological factors which affect our Christmas feelings and activities. For example, have you ever wondered why the negative behavior of teenage children is often intensified during the Christmas holidays? Of course, it doesn't always happen this way. Sometimes the thirteen- to nineteen-year-old is a "perfect joy" to have around. But often "perfect joy" is not a descriptive phrase of real behavior, but a socially accepted disguise for the tensions, hurtful forgetfulness, and on occasion, the open hostile rebellion that often characterizes the behavior of teenage kids home on Christmas vacations.

Of course, their behavior can be accounted for in many superficial ways. Maybe one's seventeen-year-old honestly believes that his freedom is being limited by a parental demand that he be home by one o'clock in the morning, that he wear shoes and socks when company visits, and that he take a bath at least once a week. And perhaps one's fourteen-year-old daughter is actually convinced that she is being unreasonably restricted by the parental notion that short-shorts are not the proper attire for the midnight Christmas Eve service, and perhaps she is equally convinced that she is being isolated when the family refuses to agree to a Holiday pot party at home. Certainly it is true that young people are presented with so many "reasonable" alternative modes of behavior these days that no one can effectively, convincingly argue against their angry claim that customary ways of doing things are needlessly restricting.

Perhaps the examples I have mentioned are too dramatic to fit the situation in your family. Perhaps your kids don't go to such lengths to express their Christmas dilemma. But the tension is there and it comes out, if not in noticeable and obvious ways then in subtle ways. For example, it is not an accident when the family car is brought home at midnight with less than half a pint of gas in the tank; a situation which obviously means that dad will be stranded on the freeway when he makes his 7 A.M. dash to the office. And when your daughter, who gets A's in high school home economics, wastes six dollars worth of cookie dough because she forgot to add the shortening, she has not suddenly suffered a lapse into premature senility. She is simply under the spell of Christmas and for teenage kids that often means painful confusion. It catapults them into a veritable roller coaster of emotion.

At lunchtime they're compliant lambs, eager to help and bright-eyed with enthusiasm. They hold out the promise of another "good old-fashioned Christmas," a Christmas just like the ones we think we remember. But by dinner time the entire picture has changed. When dad walks in after work, he can feel the tension in the household before he has even reached the kitchen. Wife and mother is humming away obviously trying to cover things over. Junior won't wake up and, after calling him ten times, somebody has to trudge upstairs after him. And when that someone finally gets him awake, he belligerently announces, "I'm not hungry." But Junior is a growing boy and somehow we can excuse his inexplicable belligerence.

But what about lovable little Sally? She's always such a joy. She has never failed to do her chores; set the table and help with the dishes. Is it an accident that tonight, the end of the first day of her Christmas vacation, she upsets the baby's milk and then tips the bowl of steaming boiled potatoes just far enough so that sleepy-eyed Junior catches one right in his lap? Are they just tense with excitement and expectations? I think not, but to demonstrate the underlying problem let me tell you about two rather dramatic episodes that display the problem in three-dimensional color.

Imprisoned by "Good" Intentions

After I had given an address to a church group on the subject of Christmas depression, a woman in the audience came up to the podium and asked if she could talk to me for a few moments. The minister offered us his study. The door was hardly closed when the woman began to weep. Her sadness and pain were genuine; it was heartbreak. When she regained her composure, she told me that her son had just been arrested for the possession of marijuana. She couldn't understand it. He was a good boy. Evidently she expected little more than sympathy from me because she was surprised when I asked for more information. She told me that her son was away at college. This was his first prolonged time away from home and everybody was looking forward to his returning for Christmas.

The family was of modest means and sending their son away

to college was a tremendous financial burden. Nevertheless, they had saved all year so that they could give him a portable TV for Christmas. Since the parents didn't own a TV themselves, they were looking forward to sharing the gift with Mike while he was home. It would be a chance for father and son to get together. They could watch pro football, share a pizza, and talk man-to-man. As she went on, it became obvious that she and her husband were trying their desperate best to live out a lifelong dream. There was no reality; no real family experience to warrant their hope that the happy reunion for which they yearned could be effected. In fact, the boy and his father had never been particularly close. They were not estranged, there was no real problem, but neither were they close. Actually the father had been too busy earning a living to spend much time with his son. And in truth, the son was a little too sensitive and quiet to bridge the gap between himself and his hard-working father. Until now, no one had been bothered by the family situation. Everything seemed to be working out all right. And then the arrest came.

There was a call from the desk sergeant at the police station and then a few tearful empty exchanges with their son over the phone. As it turned out, the son was not caught with very much pot and he was not trying to sell it. But the judge, who was known to be hard on college students, had set bail at one thousand dollars. The family couldn't possibly raise the money for a week or ten days and by that time Christmas vacation would be over. To make the parents' dilemma even worse, the sentence was two weeks in the local work house. It was a known fact that the work house officials never kept the kids locked up all day. On the contrary, they had developed an excellent work program. If school was open, college students sentenced to the work house were allowed to attend classes, study, and then return to the work house at night where they were required to do some menial chores. It was an obviously fair and humane plan.

But none of this mattered to the mother before me. She pleaded for some understanding. How could she explain this shattering episode? The answer I had to give her was painfully simple, and I feared, quite unacceptable to her. I pointed out that her son and his father had never been close and that their real objective for this Christmas was to overcome the sense of loneliness they had felt ever since their only child had gone off to college. The woman could understand all of this but what she could not see was that they were asking their son to make their dreams come true by pretending with them that somehow the spirit of Christmas had changed their family into a warm and jolly group that would have been at home with Charles Dickens' Pickwickians.

The parents could pull it off but to their son it was an intolerable, maddening burden. It was intolerable because he had been on his own and couldn't possibly go along with the old pretense. It was intolerable because it meant turning his back on the independence he had accomplished in the months he had been away. But it was maddening because at the very moment he was learning to forget the past and find his own way in life, he was beseechingly requested by his parents to reopen the wounds of the past. He was asked to be close to the father who had never had time to care. He was asked to give renewed worth and purposefulness to the empty life of his mother who had always cared too much.

And so, with unconscious purposefulness he let himself get caught with marijuana. In one simple act he disillusioned his parents, set himself free from their efforts to live out the past at his expense and found a way to affirm his young man's hope that he could "take it." Of course, it didn't have to end this way. The woman and her husband were fooling themselves about the TV. If they'd spent the one hundred and fifty dollars on a few good times for themselves they would have set their son free and as a free young man he would have most assuredly come home for Christmas.

No one is to blame in this story. They were all victims of Christmas, the season to be jolly. *They were victims of Christmas, the time when everything is supposed to be beautiful, even if we must incarcerate each other with our good intentions in order to make it so.*

Some families have achieved a high degree of sophistication in the way they handle the unfulfillable hopes aroused by Christmas. One of the best ways to both keep the hopes alive and at the same time avoid a final realization that they are unfulfillable, is to invent a family system in which one person takes on the task of providing the other members of the family with an external rationale for their internal disappointment. For example, we might consider Robin and her mother, father and two brothers. Robin was the oldest child. She had been away at college for three years so there had been plenty of time in which to create a family ritual out of her Christmas vacations. Each holiday trip home was preceded by an exchange of letters in which all parties concerned promised each other a really great Christmas.

Since preceding Christmases had been marred by family squabbles, everybody had agreed that this year it had to be different. Everybody seemed to realize that last year's arguments were silly, needless, and definitely avoidable this year, since everybody was "a little older and a little wiser." The family was seriously concerned about their holiday fights. They had a definite religious orientation toward the celebration of Christ's birth; they lived by a rather restrictive moral code, and so it seemed not only unhappy but almost sacrilegious to spend the season fighting. But this year it was to be different. After all, they had all had enough fighting, and besides, to be forewarned was to be forearmed.

The night Robin was to arrive, the home town weather was unseasonably mild. It was one of those rare Midwest December days that can be a breath of springtime in the midst of winter. The two boys were out of school and were free of homework. Mother hadn't had a "sick headache" for weeks and dad had gotten home from the office early. It seemed like a perfect night for everybody to meet Robin at the airport and then go to dinner. The plane arrived on time. Two hundred and thirty-six people out of a passenger list of two hundred and thirty-seven disembarked. Robin was number two hundred and thirty-seven. And then in front of God, a beaming airline mechanic, and at least a hundred parents of other kids arriving home from college, Robin came bouncing down the stairs, clad in a miniskirt, see-through blouse (without benefit of Bra) and an overdone coat of eye make-up. Before she had had a chance to offer up a breezy "hi," her family was galvanized in dismay. There was no mention of going out for dinner. Instead, everybody just headed for the baggage counter in strained silence. Polite caution is the phrase that can best describe the behavior of mom, dad, and the boys. But Robin was airily talkative. Once in the car, the boys started to fuss, mom quietly held her head, dad gripped the wheel like Barney Oldfield entering the final turn of the Indianapolis Five Hundred, while Robin kept clasping her hands behind her head saying, "Gee, I'm really beat."

Once home, the inevitable storm broke. Mother excused herself with a full-blown headache, the boys escalated their argument into a major fight, and dad turned on Robin as if he were the spirit of St. Paul come alive amidst Corinthian debauchery. The details of his tirade are quite unnecessary to repeat. Suffice to say that it contained all the standard phrases of any parental castigation born of righteous indignation. "How could you do this to us?"; "My God, what's the world coming to?", "Did you even think what it would mean to your parents to see you publicly exposed and indecent?", and, last but not least, "After all we've done for you, how could you do this to us?" Then it was Robin's turn to issue forth the set of clichés appropriate to the youthful stereotype she'd chosen for her Christmas season. "What's wrong with the way I'm dressed?", "All you ever think of is 'what will the neighbors think'"; "Who cares what they think?"; and, last but not least, "I've got to be me."

At this point the boys were locked into a mild but continuous argument that was to last for the remainder of the vacation. Mother was spread-eagled on the bed in her darkened bedroom with the first of a half dozen headaches that punctuated the rest of Robin's stay at home. Dad was frozen somewhere between bewilderment and rage. Robin was angrily resigned to being unappreciated for the season.

In other words, within an hour and a half of reunion, the entire family was ensconced in their usual mode of Christmas isolation. It was obviously going to be another bad Christmas, but for them their trouble appeared to have nothing to do with Christmas tension and anxiety. Christmas was going to be disappointing again, but there seemed to be a perfectly good reason for it; Robin was the reason. The fact that no one in the family had outgrown the Christmas expectations of a six-year-old remained comfortably undisclosed. It had been a narrow escape from reality. But Robin, dear little Robin and her adolescent mischief, had "saved" the day.

Of course, the people I have been describing are dramatic examples of persons in the throes of Christmas troubles, but their problems are not so very different from the less dramatic Christmas problems common to a very large segment of our population. To some extent we are all caught up in a bind by the modern Christmas. Its religious dimension is often badly misdirected. Its commercial dimension has been stretched to such a point that either the public must be immorally oversold or business must suffer huge losses and even bankruptcy. Its social dimension has engulfed the entire population in a ritual of office parties, gift exchanges and greeting card salutations that rival the extravagances of a 1920s millionaire colony during "the season." But exhausting and tiring as all of these external pressures may be, they are not primarily responsible for the pain and depression which so often characterizes Christmas. The tiring external circumstances of our celebration of the birth of Christ not only wear us down but at the same time they arouse all the hopes and fears, expectations and disappointments of our life.

The modern Christmas has ceased to be a symbol. It no longer condenses a huge variety of feelings and memories into a commonly shared celebration. It is no longer a corridor to the gentle goodness of our past. It is no longer an expression of our heritage, belief and custom. *Christmas has become a provacateur of insatiable desire.*

Before the great wars of the twentieth century showed us that our private beliefs may, when viewed from a worldwide perspective, be prejudicial to the rest of mankind, we enjoyed local customs. We were not so concerned about being provincial and narrow-minded and we could enfold ourselves in our private interpretation of the great Christmas story. Christmas used to be much more than a mere commemoration of the Savior's birth. It used to be a celebration in which we participated with our forefathers in the great events of our past. It used to be an event which enabled us to pass that heritage on to our children in a living, experiential way. There were traditional ways of doing things, accepted limits to our expectations and no way to avoid the realities of life with an exaggerated celebration.

Now, however, we live in a time when we are doubtful of our past. We are not certain that we have something good to pass on to our children. We have seen our most precious public beliefs fashioned by demagogues into instruments by which needless wars have been fought. We have grown wary of our parents' methods, their beliefs and their disciplines. The point is simply this. Christmas no longer necessarily has a unique purpose. And unless we are willing to reestablish basic Christian limits for the event it cannot have because all the provincial things it once stood for must now be objects of doubt and criticism. We are left with the shell of a tradition that has lost its core of meaning forever unless we commit ourselves to recreating that meaning. But that means opting out of "Christmas" as the great secular event of the year.

Christmas depressions can usually be avoided if we are willing to recognize the psychological pressures inherent in the secular Christmas. Christian people have sound theological reasons for joy at Christmas. But they hesitate to give up the secular Christmas because like all real joy, Christian Christmas joy must be freely shared and allowed to wax and wane. The joy of Christmas can never be possessed and it can never be purposefully sustained. Accept it, let it go, and accept it again, but never be trapped into using either secular or misguided religious maneuvers aimed at incapsulating the happiness of Christmas. It is a gift. Take it, enjoy it and give it away. Don't try to buy it.

Above all be aware that Christmas always awakens our most precious hopes. We are very vulnerable at the Christmas season and when people feel vulnerable they are apt to be anxious. But anxiety that we know about can be lived with. We don't have to try to erase it. We do not have to be victimized by the natural anxiety of the season. On the contrary, it can act as a catalyst that draws us together.

VI

Christmas Depressions for Young and Old

Consider the feelings of Mr. and Mrs. Burgmueller, an elderly couple whose daughter asked me for advice shortly after the depressing Christmas of 1971. Christmas morning was bright and crisp. The Burgmuellers' son and daughter-in-law, daughter and son-in-law and five grandchildren were in town for the holiday celebrations. Since "mother and dad" lived in a small cottage, all the kids were staying at a local motel. They planned to arrive "home" at 7 A.M. for the traditional exchange of gifts, and then the younger women were to make breakfast while the men cleaned up the house so that everybody could be ready for church at 10 o'clock that morning. It was a beautiful plan, a perfect plan. It was considerate and loving. But unfortunately the plan overlooked the effects of anxiety on old people.

Of course, the grandparents were up early and they put forth every effort to be ready for the children. But they couldn't. A flare-up of arthritis, a few misplaced articles of clothing, and just plain confusion slowed them down so that they were late. As a result, the young kids began to run out of patience and their parents, out of their wish to spare the grandparents undue pressure, overdid their discipline. The results had to be the opposite of what was planned and intended. The kids overreacted to the parents' discipline. They not only quieted down, they went into a quiet pout, and then the parents had to go out of the way to get them involved again and show some interest.

In other words, the very efforts that were meant to avoid strain, created it. Strain and disappointment were in the air. Expressions of joyful emotions had an edge to them and there was much under-the-breath direction of the children going on. Whether or not the elder Mr. and Mrs. Burgmueller actually heard these things is hard to tell, but it is absolutely certain that they felt them. The effect was just short of devastating. The harder they tried to respond "appropriately," the less able they were to respond reasonably. They become slower, a little testy, and much more confused. The family had sincerely wanted to arrive at church feeling that they had shared a few hours of loving togetherness. They wanted to feel good about themselves as a result of a genuine effort to do good for their beloved parents. Their efforts were not false; they were not self-righteous and they were not trying to overdo things.

As things turned out, however, they arrived at the church twenty minutes late. The grandchildren were disgruntled to say the least, the son and daughter were trying to be patient in their efforts to help their parents out of the car and up the church steps, but they spoiled their efforts with loudly whispered reminders to each other to "take it easy," and "now just slow down, there's no need to be in a hurry." The son-in-law and daughter-in-law stood by and tried hard to make polite small talk. They were as unaware as was everyone else of the pain that was being perpetrated on the "old folks"; the people for whom the entire effort was being made. Mrs. Burgmueller stumbled on the way up the steps and then sank into a profound state of confusion.

The church service was to have been the highpoint of the day. It was to have been a three generation participation in the ancient rite of Holy Communion. It was to have renewed their love for each other. But by the time it was over, the grandparents were depressed and physically debilitated. The children were suffering with a state of guilt that was rapidly moving them toward a demoralizing argument aimed at placing the blame for the fiasco on someone's shoulders.

But what really happened? No one was to blame; no one was at fault. The problem was simply that it was Christmas and to these good people Christmas was a time to share love, a time to go out of their way to be good to each other and a time to feel genuinely and authentically good about themselves. Certainly they cannot be faulted for these objectives. Their problem was that they simply never stopped to consider the effect their efforts would have on their parents. Somewhere in their minds they had an unquestioned fantasy of what Christmas ought to be. It was only natural for them to try to make it so. Tragically their fantasy was a product of bits and pieces of memories, TV commercials, moral obligations and traditions. However, the fantasy did not, and, because it was a fantasy, could not, include the true facts of Christmas for them in 1971. This Christmas, like so many other Christmases, for so many other well intentioned families, was a failure because it was not based on facts but on wishful thinking, hopes, dreams, and good intentions; i.e. everything but facts.

What were the facts? How could the day have been saved? The facts were that in their own way this family was victimized by their overheated notion of what Christmas should be. They just had to try and "make it good." There was no way, given their underlying idea, that they could let it be good. From this view of things, the moral of this little story is simply relax, don't try so hard. Actually, that's pretty good advice, but it still does not take into consideration the most important operative fact in this situation. The single most important fact was regression. Given an aura of tension and strain, most elderly people will find themselves pushed toward a state of psychological regression. Once this happens, they feel as if they are in psychic quicksand because the harder they try to do something about the situation, the more inept and isolated they feel. And, of course, the more inept and isolated they feel, the more regressed and childish they become.

Everyone knows that the elderly are more susceptible, more easily weakened by strain, than are younger people, but most of us do not realize the peculiar strain exerted by Christmas. Somehow, we go on thinking that grandma and grandpa will just "love every minute of it." We don't recognize, because we don't want to, that Christmas exerts a tremendous pull toward the past on older people. Just as younger people tend to look forward to something bigger and better, so older people look backward toward something bigger and better. Ironically, this backward thrust that is so much a part of Christmas for the elderly, is often taken as a sign of senility by younger people. They are either frustrated by it, (though their frustration will most often be covered over by patronizing kindness), or they will simply take the older person's emotional disengagement, the ruminating and the apparent forgetfulness, as a sorry state of affairs that they should do something about. The variety of things people think they ought to do about the situation is endless but irrespective of how they try to move the elderly out of their regression, they tragically miss the point. They simply fail to see how appropriate regression is to the elderly at Christmas. It is in going back that they try to draw us close to themselves. It is in their memories, their stories and their occasional tears that they become united with all generations.

Ironically, we ply them with gifts, usually things they know they'll never live to use, and then expect them to take pleasure in the frantic activities that keep the young comfortably oriented toward the future. They can't do it and so they fall behind. Then they are driven toward a severe, unnatural state of regression by the family's insistence that they participate in these activities at any and at all costs. Now all the massive machinery that most families have invented for dealing with mom and dad in their "old age" must swing into action. Pathetically, in their attempt to avoid the touching memories of age; in their well intentioned efforts to stifle the bittersweet sadness of youth grown old, good families create the painful loneliness of senility.

Spare Us the Truth

And why do we do it? We do it because we cannot live with regression in someone else if it threatens to expose the full meaning that Christmas actually has for us all. Christmas is a time of aroused hopefulness for all of us but since some of those hopes can never be fulfilled, we turn away from them. The young have the energy, the time and the ignorance necessary to deny the impossibility of Christmas dreams, but the old have little energy, no time and few illusions with which to protect themselves from the facts of life. And so the gifts we bring and the activities we plan seem to have a paradoxical if not an inexplicable effect. They arouse the cherished memories of the past but because they are memories which the old have come to terms with and which the young still avoid, there can be no sharing. The old must be stifled.

The inevitable results are that the very things with which we hoped to give pleasure turn out to increase the isolation of age. Then the elderly must, out of fear and loneliness, flee to debilitating regression. They are hurt because they are not allowed to include themselves in their children's lives, and their children are frustrated, puzzled, probably angry and most assuredly guilty because somehow they sense that it was their own private fears that prevented them from listening rather than planning new activities; from sharing rather than just giving, and from participating in the quiet honesty of age rather than hanging on to the strained illusions and denials of youth.

Depression in the elderly at Christmas time is spelled loneliness, but it does not necessarily have anything to do with being alone. Depression for the aged is the result of the isolation of regression, a self-imposed loneliness which, though painful, is preferable to the unbearable sense of separation that an old man or woman must feel when they are forced to live in a world which on the one hand arouses their hopes and dreams and on the other hand denies them a chance to share themselves; to be included in the one way that is most meaningful to them.

The simple ghastly truth was dramatically presented to me a few years ago when I learned about a seventy-six-year-old man who had been in good mental and physical health until Christmas. He lived alone, took good care of himself, and was known to have a great many friends who enjoyed his endless willingness to listen to their accounts of their busy days in exchange for a few of his stories of days gone by. Then the Christmas of 1970 approached and someone got the great idea that grandpa should be included in the fun. Unhappily that meant that grandpa was to be flown a thousand miles from his home town where he could be included in a swirl of activities that were simply too much for him. Including grandpa in the fun meant depriving him of his right to include someone in his fun. But in January of 1971 everybody was glad they had made the effort because right after Christmas grandpa retired to a nursing home.

When the old man arrived at our hospital for a psychiatric work-up, we found him unable to feed, bathe, or dress himself. He seldom spoke but from his relatives we gradually learned that there had been a precipitous change in his behavior and outlook on life when he was denied the opportunity to spend his own money for a doll he wanted to purchase for a new baby in the family. When I last saw this once dignified, independent man, he was rocking back and forth on the porch of the hospital, clutching a Bible to his breast. Everybody thought he had turned to religion in his last days. But I knew better. He had never turned away from the faith of his fathers, but having been unwittingly deprived of an opportunity to share himself in a way that was appropriate to his years, he had been forced into a depressing regression. To him the Bible was no longer the book of faith it had been to him in former years. It was a baby doll, the doll he had wanted to give when he was still a man. But thanks to a well intentioned but uninformed family's efforts to include him in their "fun," he was now the child he had once sought to please.

It is not an accident that Christmas often draws extreme age and extreme youth together. Grandma can always quiet the screaming toddler and not a few grandpas have an almost magical way of diverting the rambunctious activities of their grandsons into constructive avenues. The union of young and old at Christmas is not an accident because more often than not they share a common problem. Often they are strangely drawn together because they intuitively sense that they both yearn for relief from the strain of "having a good time." Children, particularly the very young, are considered to be the essence of Christmas, the real reason for it all. But it is a plain, simple and undeniable truth that no child can sustain the strain of the pre-Christmas build-up and the exhaustion associated with Christmas Eve and Christmas Day and have anything like a good time. When we add to this dismal scene the fact that most parents are so concerned about their own undisciplined behavior that they cannot effectively govern even the basic aspects of their child's life, it becomes apparent that the child is in deep trouble at Christmas. Consider the absurdity of a mother losing her temper and screaming at a five-year-old child whose mind has been reduced to the mentality of an eighteen-month-old baby because he has, in the name of having a good time Christmas shopping, been deprived of the afternoon nap he has been accustomed to taking.

Every parent knows that when children are tired they regress. But few seem to realize that the angry protests which children raise against the reasonable discipline one must exert if collapse is to be avoided, is a normal, reasonable attempt on the child's part to deny his regressed state; i.e. to show that he can stay up as late as the adults. If parents understood this they would certainly take effective action rather than shout, threaten, coax, or bully a child who, for sheer lack of rest, is spiraling downward toward a complete loss of self-esteem and physical exhaustion. The process is so obvious, so common, and so hurtful that one must either conclude that we live in a nation of sadistic parents or that the nation's parents are so spellbound by the web of Christmas that they cannot use their common sense in handling their children. I definitely prefer the latter explanation of the holiday chaos that more often than not leads children, the playful, joyful little tots who are supposed to enjoy the holiday more than anyone, to the same humiliating state of regression so frequently experienced by their elders.

It is difficult to think of children as being depressed. They may seem sad to us or strangely quiet or we may recognize that they are eating poorly and having a difficult time sleeping. But it seldom occurs to us that these are typical symptoms of depression. Suffice to say that children can be and are often depressed. And their depression is every bit as painful and probably more serious than the depressions of adulthood. Adults have a frame of reference built up over years of experience that can enable them to weather a depression. But children have no such frame of reference. They have no experience to rely on. Consequently, they experience their bouts with depression as total disappointments with themselves. When we add to these considerations the fact that depression at Christmas time is likely to be completely overlooked by the adults to whom a child might ordinarily turn for help, we can see that the condition of a child in the throes of a fatiguing, demoralizing Christmas depression is desperate. The child is fortunate if he can emerge from it without permanent damage. But often they are not fortunate and the seeds of deep distrust of one's ability to sustain one's self-esteem take root.

Children, Santa Claus and gifts, are hallmarks of Christmas embraced by all of us. It is true that many families are concerned lest the Santa Claus business be carried too far and turn into the insulting deception that the Stork story once was. But who would want to give up the idea of freely giving to the ones we love the most, our children? And who wants to be completely reasonable about it? A festival occasion is hardly festive if everyone is going to be totally sensible about things. It is probably true that the most reasonable thing one can do with a great festival is to relax one's sense of responsibility and hard reason. The joy of the occasion is not, however, increased by senselessness.

The things I have been saying about Christmas are in no way meant to dampen the holiday spirit. I'm not suggesting that we return to the old Puritan tradition of sending the town crier around on December 25th saying, "No Christmas today." I am only suggesting that a degree of insight into the mammoth event into which the modern Christmas has grown may enable us to apply an underlying rationale to our conduct that will spare us from turning a potentially joyful occasion into a depressing celebration of ambivalence and pain.

Ambivalence, that state of mind in which one cannot make up one's mind about anything, is the expected norm for children from age ten to thirteen. Of course, kids at all ages suffer with this problem because they are all growing. They see the world and themselves a little differently every day of their lives, so it is only natural for them not to feel sure or even reasonably certain about anything. Sometimes their confusion becomes almost too much to bear and then they find themselves on the edge of personal chaos. It is at these times that children will throw themselves with devotion into almost any idea, cause, or activity. I do not want to depreciate either the fervor or the causes to which young people give themselves. It would be helpful, however, if the adults whom children need for guidance could realize that much of the time both the cause and the fervor are merely a frantic attempt to escape the underlying uncertainty of childish ambivalence.

Christmas brings the problem to focus. Consider, for example, the plight of Andy, a thirteen-year-old who had saved up fifty dollars which his parents had offered to match so that he could have a ten-speed bike for Christmas. Andy had his heart set on the bike. It took him months to save up his part of the cost but he did it. Now mom and dad, true to their word, put up the other fifty dollars and off they went to the local bike shop to pick out the best machine a one hundred dollar bill would buy. The days that remained before Christmas, the time agreed upon to present the bike, were difficult ones for Andy. He was excited, a little irritable, and talked of nothing other than what he'd do when he got his bike.

Christmas morning went off without a hitch and Andy was out of the house and on the streets before anyone had time to get mad at him for not helping clean up. But just an hour later Andy's parents got a telephone call from a neighbor. There had been an accident. Andy wasn't hurt but the bike was bent out of shape almost as badly as was Andy's pride. The neighbor suggested that the parents come and help him get home. After the initial fright of the situation was surmounted, everybody, both parents and son, turned their attention to the question, "How could it happen?" Andy was a good, careful and experienced rider. He had wracked up the bike on a quiet side street. There was no traffic, no ice on the pavement, no snapping dogs to account for the fact that he had run headlong into a forty-foot oak tree.

The psychiatrist who told me the story, (he was the next-door neighbor), got a few more facts. He learned that in the time Andy had been away, he had traveled twelve miles to the other side of the subdivision. The "accident" happened when he was half of the way back home. In other words, Andy had covered eighteen miles in an hour. More importantly, however, was the fact that Andy was apparently not just joyriding around. It was never openly admitted but it was almost certain that Andy was intent on riding by the home of a friend in the hope that he might just happen to have a chance to show off his bike. And the friend just happened to be a girl.

None of these facts accounted for the accident. The accident just couldn't have been simply an accident. When Andy was questioned, all anybody learned was, "I don't know what happened. I just looked up and there was this tree comin' at me."

His answer, though obviously sincere, just wasn't adequate. Unhappily, the adequate answer was one that Andy's parents would never have believed. They couldn't have believed the real answer because they were completely unaware of the ambivalence Andy felt about getting his bike. And how could they have been aware of it? After all, he was almost frantically devoted to getting it and after all, doesn't every thirteen-year-old boy want a bike? The answer is yes on both accounts but it is also true that the cocksure thirteen-year-old is covering up a basic sense of ambivalence, a painful basic sense of indecision that is enormously intensified by Christmas.

And what are they ambivalent about? They are ambivalent about everything, but mostly about freedom. On the one hand, they angrily demand it and on the other hand they destroy the very means of achieving it. Andy's ride was much more than a simple exercise of boyish enthusiasm. It was a dramatic break for freedom. At last he had a real means to be on his own. It was not just talk or a plan anymore. Now he could be away from home; out of sight and sound of the old restraints. But once he reached out and took his freedom he found that he was also cut off from the safety of his home. He loved his bike and he wanted the freedom it gave him, but the fear that arose in him as he found himself riding home after a secretive few moments with his first girl took him by complete surprise.

The accident was not an accident at all. It was a boy's way of responding to the cold hand of anxiety that always follows new freedom and first love. But there had to have been other firsts in Andy's life. There had been a first time to go to the movies alone, a first party, and even long bike rides on his brother's bike. But on these other occasions Andy was not thirteen, and not so torn within himself. And these other times had never happened at Christmas. Christmas had heightened his ambivalence because it both aroused his child's delight and also offered him a chance to step out of a boy's role and move toward young manhood. Probably most significant of all, Christmas deprived Andy of sensitive parents with whom to talk, i.e. parents who would have somehow realized that things were not quite right and would have intuitively placed restraints on his first excursions. Andy's parents were good people but they didn't understand what Christmas does to thirteen-year-old boys so the time to be jolly became the time to be sorry. Gratefully, it did not have to become a time for mourning. Andy was off the hook simply by bending up his bike but when the problem is sufficiently intense, bent bikes are not enough and more serious injuries must occur.

Christmas Shopping

To close these chapters on the psychological problems of Christmas, I must write briefly on the one remaining activity of the Christmas season that summarizes all that I have said; Christmas shopping. Christmas shopping symbolizes the anxious quality of the holiday. It typifies the depressing regressiveness of the season as well as our exhausting self-defeating attempts to make the system work. Of course, Christmas shopping can be fun but the simple fact is that for most people it is not. There is very little fun in joining a mob scene at the local shopping center in order to pay an inflated price for a gift which the receiver probably doesn't need and may not even want.

Again let me make it clear that I realize that there are many exceptions to this dismal picture. The exceptions, however, have something in common. Buying a particular gift for a loved one whose wishes and needs are known to one is not what I call "Christmas shopping." Christmas shopping to me is a massive effort to buy something for everybody on a list composed of friends, relatives, and business acquaintances that one has made up on the basis of one's own receipts the previous Christmas. The activity I have in mind is not a pleasure characterized by a spur of the moment purchase because just the right thing for Tom or Mary has caught one's eye. Nor is it a relaxed hour of browsing around for something one would really like to give a friend or loved one. This kind of buying implies a freedom to choose; even the freedom to not give if the right thing doesn't turn up. But "Christmas shopping" leaves no time for the pleasure of selection and no freedom to decide. The massive shopping that accounts for endless traffic jams, packed crowds of people milling around in stores that pipe in Christmas music (for the same reason that farmers play Mantovani in their cow barns) is a carefully manipulated exercise in mob psychology.

This kind of buying has nothing to do with sharing. It has little to do with pleasure of any kind except perhaps the relief of getting it done. The psychology that underlies the manipulated buying, the massive con job that Christmas buying has become, concerns all the negative factors we have been talking about. First, we are carefully seduced into participating in a holiday that apparently has lost all of its boundaries, all of its special meaning and all of its essential tradition. Having succumbed, we are set up for frayed nerves on the one hand and we are bombarded with comforting memories on the other hand. These two things together both push us and pull us toward the regressive process which we fear. If we regress we will buy like frightened, spoiled children and if we resist regression we are liable to spend even more, but we will carefully buy things that tend to prove to ourselves that we are controlled, sophisticated people. Often the difference boils down to spending too much at Sears and Roebuck or spending too much at Abercrombie and Fitch.

When we consider compulsive Christmas buying in this light it becomes clear that we are really talking about a psychological symptom, i.e. a psychological maneuver that both hides feelings that make us uncomfortable, and at the same time enables us to express those things in a disguised way. In other words, Christmas arouses uncomfortable feelings which we must avoid. We feel pushed toward the past which, unless we have come to accept both its pain and joy, we feel constrained to resist. When we add to this picture the fact that the pressure of the event keeps up relentlessly for two and one-half to three months it becomes obvious why we are eventually so fatigued that we are driven to extraordinary means of denying our regressed state. Buying, wild thoughtless buying so that we can check off names on our list like a good child who has done his chores, is carefully presented to us as the best of all possible means of relieving this unbearable pressure.

But of course, it doesn't work. Like any psychological symptom, it is a means by which we hope to bring relief to ourselves that inevitably backfires and becomes a source of anxiety in and of itself. For example, the first one hundred dollars spent may feel somewhat satisfying. But when we spend the second one hundred dollars in the hope of gaining complete relief we begin to get anxious about the money we are spending. We never seem to be able to put two and two together; to back off and see that if we really want to decrease our anxiety all we have to do is pare down Christmas to a comprehensible celebration that gives us a chance to express our joy rather than wear ourselves into depression.

So why don't we do it? We don't because we get caught up in the massive influence of the season to be jolly. To avoid it, all we need is a little insight and an honest desire to once again make Christmas an occasion of joy and goodwill, a time when we draw each other into our lives; a time for a renewed realization that the miracle of Bethlehem began in lowly, common circumstances. The only person who laid plans and spent money on the occasion was Herod, a threatened man driven to destroy the magic of love freely given.

It is tempting to close these chapters on Christmas depression with a cheering restatement of the Christian message. God incarnate in man, God born that man might be reborn, this is good news indeed. Unfortunately good news does not psychologically alter people after they have been drawn into the throes of depression. It is also good news that God wants us to live with healthy bodies. God's desire is the same even after twenty years of overeating, drinking and smoking have ruined our health. So it is with the Christmas message. The time to apply that message is *before* we have so mismanaged the circumstances and the emotions of the season that we are too depressed to be psychologically affected by *"good news."*

VII

A Bundle of Joy and a Depression

Mary Ann Blyth was a 23-year-old new mother. The delivery had gone well, the baby was healthy, her husband was pleased and proud and everybody was happy except Mary Ann. At first the family made all kinds of excuses for her weeping, her disenchantment with the baby and her pessimism, but eventually they had to admit that she was depressed. Mary Ann had everything going for her. She came from an upper middle class home; had been raised in affluence but had also known hard work. She was not spoiled. Her husband was a successful young lawyer who loved his wife and wanted a family. She had health, wealth, a beautiful baby and a depression.

Depression May Be Unavoidable

I did the psychiatric work-up and after going over the details of her past and present life, her dreams and fantasies, her emotions and her rationale, I found nothing to warrant her being depressed. I found nothing, except the fact that Mary Ann had

111

just been through one of those deeply moving natural events of life that have a way of arousing one's awareness of the dark side of existence. The very idea that depression may be an unavoidable natural aspect of life runs absolutely contrary to the popular, highly publicized notion that anything which is seriously uncomfortable can and should be changed, i.e. made an OK part of ourselves or thought through to a "positive" conclusion. Unfortunately, I have to take exception to this popular notion because it simply isn't true. Depression is not always avoidable. Sometimes it is an integral part of life.

Obviously no one wants to believe that there are depressing times in life which we cannot avoid or overcome. We all resist this knowledge and that brings me to a second important aspect of natural depression. Depression is a fact of life which we actually resist knowing about. There are a great many people who would disagree with me on this matter. To many people it doesn't seem right to talk about a "naturally depressing" event and it makes even less sense to suggest that people choose to be blind to this kind of depression. To some psychologists and not a few theologians, life "should be beautiful," or at least free of depression, and if it isn't something must be wrong. Given this philosophy, it follows quite naturally that we will want to find the trouble and do something about it.

Natural Depression

This sunny, appealing, "positive" view of human psychology simply denies the essential perversity of human nature, physical and psychological. For example, childbirth is probably the most natural event in any woman's life and certainly I would not want to deny the essential beauty of the event. But having delivered a number of mothers, I can assure the reader that this natural event is usually physically uncomfortable for the mother, and perhaps for the baby, and it is often downright painful. In other words, it is quite natural for the most natural event of life to be somewhat painful.

The same thing can be said of the psychology of natural events. As we all know, young people are psychologically driven toward the creation of new life. It is also true that when that life comes into being it is likely to cause some kind of psychological pain and depression. This fact is no less true because some young people are obliged to deny their feelings when talking to middle-aged or older friends and relatives who simply cannot imagine that a new baby can be experienced as a depressing reality rather than a "bundle of joy." It is true that much can be done to alleviate this painful aspect of birth and other natural events, but, contrary to the desire which most people have to deny unhappiness, a residue of discomfort is always present.

Pain and sadness are always a part of great events because they are the milestones that mark our progress through life. They tell us that we must move on away from the comfortable past toward acceptance of an unfamiliar future. There is no way to go on to new things, more mature objectives and relationships, until we have given up old things. And giving up is *always* painful. But it is depressing only when the loss of the past cannot be openly admitted and mourned. *Sadness that is denied produces depression because it is a basic restriction of our freedom. It is a limitation for which we will eventually hate ourselves no matter how comforting it may seem at the moment.*

Life Can Be Beautiful — and Depressing

This is why I take such sharp issue with the "life can be beautiful" people. They increase our natural resistance to realizing the loss that is inherent in going through the stages of life, and thereby make it more difficult for us to mourn the loss and get it over with. They increase our feeling that there is something wrong with us if we find ourselves sad at a time of birth, a time when new life has been born. And because we think there is something wrong with us we are more liable to deny our sadness. We are liable to use our happiness as a means of hiding our sadness. Thus, our happiness will become strained and artificial; our sadness will remain naggingly with us and never yield to growth.

Birth Is a Loss?

At this point the reader may wonder what kind of loss is involved in childbirth. Obviously if the family is unable to support a new baby, or if the parents are ill, or if it is predicted that the child will be unhealthy, there is good external reason for being depressed. That is, in these circumstances one would have to give up one's hopes and dreams for a healthy child born into an adequately supportive family. But to a significant extent the same conditions exist even when there is no unhealth involved and there is no family problem. Every child is, to one degree or another, expected to be something that it cannot possibly be. Unconsciously we expect our child to be beautiful, healthy, talented, intelligent, and loving. There is no way to avoid these expectations. They are a natural, healthy part of mental life. But by the same token there is no way for parents to avoid the disappointment that is associated with these expectations.

Unfortunately, the "life can be beautiful" people are in such a commanding position in the matter of childbirth that it is almost impossible for a mother or a father to express their disappointment with a child. They cannot talk to themselves or between themselves, or to their parents or their friends about their disappointment. If they were to do so it would be inevitably interpreted as a lack of love and caring on their part. Worst of all, it would probably be laughed off and brushed aside. So the expectations we have for a child must be frustrated and that frustration must go either unrecognized or borne alone. In either case the essential task of giving up one's naturally unrealistic expectations cannot be accomplished. Mourning cannot go on; the hopes and desires that were such a natural part of life before birth cannot give way to genuine enjoyment of the real child that emerges after birth.

I hope it is apparent by this time that the seemingly unnatural depression which many mothers feel after birth is usually a very natural phenomenon. (Of course, I am not overlooking the possibility of mental illness.) Post partum depression is associated with the lonely realization of profound loss which birth takes a mother through. It is a loss of an individual which has been part of oneself in the most intimate of all possible relationships. New life begins with a cleavage of bodies, a separation of souls. It is true that some women seem to experience the separation inherent in birth as a passing and even inconsequential matter relative to the joy of having delivered a new human being into the world. But all women are aware of a sense of loss at one time or another after birth.

To particularly sensitive women, women who have intuitively experienced the pregnant state as the most meaningful and purposeful time of their life, the loss inherent in birth can mobilize and focus memories on other losses. To such women birth can quite naturally become a time of losing, of failure. Tragically, such a woman will more than likely end up depressed rather than openly sad for a few days or weeks. She will end up depressed because without help and understanding she will have to tell herself that she has nothing to be sad about. She will have to believe that there is something wrong with her for feeling sad.

And, of course, she will eventually hate herself for denying herself the right to be sad. If she should become the victim of a relative, a minister, a doctor or a friend who is convinced that "having a baby is just the most beautiful thing in the world" she will feel obliged to deny whatever apprehension, concern and sadness she may have. Thus, the pleasant but thoughtless words of a well-meaning friend become incarcerating.

Of course I'm not suggesting that we approach childbirth expecting to be sad. We can't. It isn't natural. It is natural to resist a realization of the sadness that is involved. But by the same token we need not be taken by complete surprise when it hits us. Understanding the fact that sadness may be a natural part of the greatest event of life can reduce our resistance to accepting that sadness when it becomes an actual part of our life. And the less we resist the sadness; the more freedom we give ourselves to feel and express the full range of our emotions, the less probable it is that we will be depressed. Depression is directly related to our resistance to owning up to sadness. The more we resist the more angry we will be with ourselves and the more depressed we will be.

Depression Is an Aspect of Growth

Because depression is the result of our resisting an expression of sadness and the giving up that is involved in birth, it is an aspect of growth. Here I must restate a self-evident fact that almost no one believes. Psychological growth is only partially a matter of mental enrichment, i.e. an increase in our mastery of complexity and an increase in our ability to do more with less effort. The other part of growth is a matter of giving up old ways of thinking and acting which are incompatible with new thoughts and actions. In a sense, (there are exceptions), we do not grow by adding to our personality. We grow by replacing aspects of our personality. One cannot take a new and better route to work in the morning without deciding not to take the old route. Nor can one grow toward mature love within a marriage and at the same time work for the playful bliss of puppy love. We don't like to think that there are limits to our human potential. I personally feel that there are very few real limits to what we can become, but there are very sharp limits to what we can become without giving up something of what we have been. Some of the most seductive and appealing psychological systems of our time are based on the notion that we can and should be able to be all things at all times. If these philosophies of "growth" and potential were merely topics of discussion, they might well be a source of education. Unfortunately, they have become a rationale for action.

Eventually people who have been seduced into believing that growth is a mere matter of fulfillment without deprivation will be yanked back into the barbed wire confines of human existence. They will learn via their own pain that "living together" is not a marriage; that one cannot have an "open marriage" and at the same time know love and devotion; that one cannot wander through school or work and at the same time know the excitement of excellence; and that one cannot know freedom, meaning, and purpose without freely accepting a frame of reference within which to live. Eventually they will know that at least half of growing is a matter of giving up. I only hope that when disillusionment strikes, as it surely will, a few of these good people will be open to the message of the Christian faith.

VIII

Depression and
the Prime of Life

Peter Johnson had just turned 42 when he decided to come in and consult me about his depression. He was a professional man who, to all outward appearances, had nothing to be depressed about. His wife was a kind, gentle, intelligent woman who loved him very much. His children were, by most standards, doing well and seemed even more happy with home than most young adults. And last but not least, he made $60,000 a year and that gave the Johnson family considerable freedom.

Like so many men who were born during the great economic depression of the late Twenties and early Thirties, Peter Johnson had spent the first fifteen to twenty years of his life not daring to hope for "real success." His chance came with the G.I. Bill of Rights after World War II. In college and graduate school he discovered he had a talent for his field that made it realistic for him to dream of becoming the successful, accomplished man he had always secretly wanted to be.

Of course success to Peter Johnson meant material goods; cars, a big house, private plane lessons and private schools for the kids;

but more importantly it meant "being somebody." It meant recognition and that warm good feeling that one is important, deferred to and special. I want to emphasize, however, that this man's desire for success was not pompous or selfish or totally unrealistic. He simply wanted "to be somebody."

As we might expect, Mr. Johnson was not resigned to being depressed. He was angry and ashamed of his depression because he had assumed that it was all due to his having let "success go to his head." Specifically speaking, he meant that "success" was responsible for his "running around." He reasoned that if he were still fighting to get to the top in his profession he would never have had time to "chase after women." And he assumed that if he hadn't gotten involved in clandestine affairs he would have no cause to be depressed because then he would still have his wife's love and his children's admiration. As it was, it seemed that everything worthwhile and good and meaningful was gone. And Peter Johnson was angrily, unreservedly depressed about it.

Insight and Hard Work May Not Help

The reader may notice that given the story as it was told to me by Mr. Johnson, his depression was largely a matter of misunderstanding and misusing external circumstances. That is, I could just as easily have talked about this man's trouble in the chapters on vacation and Christmas depressions. This is the way it appears because this is the way the patient chose to see it. Actually, however, his depression was not even remotely related to his "running around." Social and sexual promiscuity were merely the results of his depression. To him these results were terribly depressing, but in fact he was not nearly as depressed as he would have been if he had not been able to distract himself from the real depression that had plagued him for months prior to his first incident of "stepping out." He would have felt worse if he had not been able to account for his problem in terms of external results rather than an internal condition because the internal condition was a "natural depression." It was a depression associated with being in the prime of life, successful, and everything that he had hoped to be.

The basic problem was one of those natural depressions associated with a time of life, a time of arriving, of "being somebody." The idea of being the victim of a depression which could not be overcome with insight and hard work was almost intolerable to this action-oriented, do-something-positive-about-everything man. But paradoxically, the more he tried to do something about his depression, the more resolutions and promises and apologies he made, the worse he felt. It almost seemed that the harder he tried to live the honest, clean life he had known for the first thirty-eight years of his life, the sooner he felt irresistibly pulled back to his immorality. He felt "possessed."

Success Can Be Depressing

Unfortunately his pastor and fellow churchmen were very little help to him. Of course news of his affairs had leaked out, and of course everybody at church assumed that this was the source of his trouble. They counselled and advised and prayed that he would give up his destructive ways and get right with God. Their concern and their attempts to be helpful were well intended, but since they dealt with the results of this man's problem rather than the problem itself, they could not succeed. Mr. Johnson's problem was depression that had started months before he did anything immoral.

But why was he depressed and why did he go down the road of promiscuity? He was depressed about being a success. Like many of us he had spent years dreaming of it. He hoped for it and worked for it. It was inevitable that over the years his dreams and efforts would pick up a slightly unreal quality. In a most natural way his success gradually became equated with influence, freedom from worry and "the good life." By and large, however, his hopes were not wildly unreal. Given his profession, his talent and the success-oriented society in which we all live, they were mostly attainable. Mr. Johnson's trouble was not that he wanted more than he could achieve. His trouble was that he achieved almost every goal he had set for himself only to face the fact that his goals were painfully unsatisfying. Of course some people never have Mr. Johnson's trouble. Every time they reach a realization that the goals for which they have been striving are basically unsatisfying, they simply invent new and more difficult goals to achieve. But Mr. Johnson was too sensitive a man to do that. He had worked for twenty years to become an admirable success only to find out that he was the only one who really cared very much about it. His friends were indeed impressed with his yearly new car, big suburban home, freedom to travel, and his generous pledge to the church, but no one respected him for it and certainly no one loved him for it. He was on top of the world, king of the hill, and yet no one seemed anxious to change places with him. Mr. Johnson was disillusioned and frustrated beyond endurance.

In the middle of Chapter II, I attempted to help the reader understand the inner workings of depression, i.e. self-hate. I have not referred each and every example back to this discussion, but Mr. Johnson is a classic example of depression predicated on hopelessness, frustration, regression to childish behavior and a childish way of handling psychological problems, i.e. identification with the frustrating person. If you have forgotten this sequence of events, glance through the last part of Chapter II again.

I have already described just how frustrated and disillusioned Mr. Johnson was. It almost goes without saying that since no one understood or even saw a reason for understanding his problem in any way other than superficial, moral terms, he was terribly alone and so he regressed. Having regressed, he sought relief from his frustration and loneliness by identifying; i.e. becoming like the people who had frustrated him. Since he could not be close to them as an admired adult, he regressed and then overcame his sense of aloneness with one of the most effective and common methods of childhood. He became one with the people who frustrated him by psychologically gobbling them up.

If you are having a hard time understanding why a person would try to overcome separation and loneliness by becoming like the very people who have been rejecting, look at it this way. It is as if the person said to himself, "They (the rejector) will love me if I hate myself the way they hate me." Remember, the person is thinking from a regressed, childlike frame of reference. Like a child, they don't see that there may be alternative ways of regaining a sense of union with the person that had rejected them. A child cannot live without, in one way or another, feeling close to those few people upon whom it must rely for the basic necessities of life. This is why people who have regressed do such apparently strange things. They do those strange things because they are locked into a very narrow, childlike frame of reference from which they cannot look at all the alternatives which would be apparent to any person operating on an adult level. Becoming like the person who has rejected one is a method of overcoming estrangement as ancient as mankind. But somewhere in everybody's mind there is a realm of thought and idea where we honestly believe that we may become that which we psychologically take inside of ourselves. (Of course, in primitive societies people literally ate that which they wanted to become.)

Depression and the Middle-aged Kid

Now I must introduce the reader to a twist in this sequence of events that is very important and quite common. If you recall, the unruly little girl of Chapter II regressed, identified with her mother and that was all there was to it. She now complained about herself the same way her mother had complained about her. Mother thought she was being a "perfect little lady," and so the child felt accepted and the mother was pleased. Actually Mr. Johnson went through short periods of time in which he acted this way. He'd reform and be a "good boy" but he couldn't carry it off for very long. Many adults, particularly aggressive, capable men and women, just can't settle for this. They can't settle for acceptance predicated on self-rejection and hatred. The sequence is still frustration, regression and identification, but instead of identifying with the critical, "rejecting" adults in their world, they identify with the rebellious young people they see around them. They do this because we live in a youth-oriented society.

In our world young people are the rejectors. They are the people who make us take stock of ourselves and wonder if it's all worthwhile. Youth in fact sets the tone of our society. All moralizing aside, most middle-aged people are just plain jealous of the "apparent freedom" most kids have today. And they are furious when they cannot get young people to admire them for their driven, thoughtless devotion to "success." In our world it is young people who are most apt to make us feel disillusioned and alone. Hence a capable professional man, Mr. Johnson, can end up flaunting, bragging and rebelling like a person less than half his age. Teenagers are the isolators, the frustrators; they are the people who make us feel alienated; the people with whom most adults unconsciously want to be close.

To an external observer it may look as if a person like Mr.

Johnson has simply taken leave of his good senses. But to the person who is going through all of this, their behavior makes absolute sense. They feel relieved, rejuvenated and sensible. Don't be surprised to find that such a person has developed a rather complete philosophy to support his adolescent action. Given the shapeless condition of our social morals, it is quite easy to make promiscuity, the destruction of relationships that have been built up over decades, and the abandonment of home and work look like a sensible break for new freedom. However, the simple truth is they cannot give up what they are doing because it is a way out of a gnawing, debilitating, middle age success depression.

What to do about it? If this state of affairs describes you to some degree, then don't fool yourself. Get someone to talk to and start owning up to the empty disappointment that is always the dark side of success. If you know someone like this then be sure you are thinking and talking from a realization of the real facts. Be careful you are not in fact dealing with your own defensiveness. Remember, no matter how much sense the middle-aged jock in a foreign sports car accompanied by a beautiful young girl may make, relative to what he has given up his actions are pathetic. Stop and think for a minute about what he, or she, says they want. They want excitement, freedom and love with "no strings attached." Haven't you seen or heard that before? Of course, it's right out of the thought and actions of your teenage son or daughter who will gladly promise you love and affection if you will let them have a party for their friends. Think about the last time you went through that. You worked for forty-eight hours getting things ready, they had a good time and no one remembered to say "Thanks." In kids it's normal. In an adult it's a sign of depression, all sophisticated arguments notwithstanding. Remember, working with such a person is no excuse to dive headlong into a pool of reassuring moralizing and righteous recrimination. *What is needed is understanding; understanding of the loss of hopes and dreams that success always involves. What is needed is an understanding of the deep yearning for companionship that goes with this kind of disillusionment.*

IX

Anniversaries, Birthdays —and Depression

Let me tell you about a woman who retired from work and did *not* get depressed. She had worked for the same company for 58 years. Like so many people of an earlier generation, she began work out of sheer necessity. She was twelve years old when her company offered her a job after her father had been killed while driving a team of horses across a railroad track. Ruth was the oldest of five children whom her mother had to support. So it goes without saying that her job was vitally important to her right from the beginning. As the years passed, there came a time when she was relieved of her duties to her brothers and sisters. She could have given up work when she married but by this time she was a skilled and valued employee. Her husband admired her ability and had no desire for her to quit her job. On two occasions she took off six months to have a baby.

If anybody could be considered a setup for depression upon retirement, it was Ruth. Work was central in her life. She was good at it and she loved it. Privately her friends worried that she would be at a "total loss to know what to do with herself" after retirement. But in fact, the retirement party came and went without any indication of depression. Ruth shed a few tears but then so did the young employees whom she was leaving. She went through a period of reorganization that included a few blue Mondays, but nothing that could be called depression. She was never bothered by that peculiar sense of fatigue, worthlessness and self-depreciation that is so characteristic of depression. In a short while she got her ideas about her future together. She increased her work at church, read more, and she and her husband took a few trips together. Ruth did a lot of things after retirement that she couldn't have done while she was working, but I am sure that the things she did, while helpful, were not the reason she remained free from depression. Ruth was not only free from depression, she just plain lived more after retirement.

Meaningful Work vs. Meaningful People Who Work

Many people become depressed at the close of a lifetime of work because they experience an intolerable loss; a loss so great they cannot accept it, mourn it, and get over it. These are people who have derived the meaning and purpose of life from their work. They are people whose importance as human beings has been dependent on their work. Consequently, when work is denied them they have no way of finding meaning in their life. Ruth was not this kind of person. Work was important to her because she found in it an opportunity to express the deep sense of pride she felt about herself independent of her work. In other words, to Ruth, work was a chance to express the goodness she felt about herself. Work did not give her a sense of basic goodness. It never imparted meaning and purpose to her life. On the contrary, she imparted purpose and meaning to her work.

The difference in these two positions is of the utmost importance when we consider depression associated with an anniversary; an occasion that marks time for us and separates the past from the future. In the matter of retirement, an anniversary of sorts, a person who needs work in order to feel that their life is important will probably get depressed. But a person who imparts purpose and meaning to work is free to work or not to work. They are free to let go. They may miss it, they may even mourn its loss for a time, but they will not end up feeling that they aren't "worth much" without scheduled, income-producing labor. The same thing can be said of women whose work is with a family and a home. If the children give meaning to her life, she'll suffer a great loss when they leave. She may end up feeling like she's "unneeded and worthless." If, however, children and a home are an opportunity to express the worthwhileness she attributes to her own life, then their loss, while difficult, will simply mean that she must seek new people and tasks to enliven her life.

Let me put this matter in a little different way. Anniversaries (and retirement is only an example of an anniversary) punctuate time for us. They always involve a loss for us because they bring us to a realization that part of life is over. Young people graduating from high school must face the fact that they can never be high school kids again, and men and women facing retirement must realize the fact that they can never be 40, or 60, or even 65 again. Unconsciously (and sometimes quite consciously) anniversaries signify a loss of a significant part of life. This is why people so frequently lie about their age. They simply can't own up to loss. Still, this in itself is not necessarily depressing. It is a loss that can be mourned and gotten over. *The thing that is depressing about anniversaries is that they inevitably deprive us of some aspect of the basic illusions we all have about life, illusions which we resist acknowledging.*

None of us comes even close to being realistic about life. We all embrace some basic assumptions which, because we don't want to examine them, we rarely talk about. I've already mentioned one such illusion, i.e. the idea that work gives meaning and purpose to life. But there are others. Most people really don't believe that they are ever going to die. (Incidentally, people who talk about dying all the time usually believe they are going to live forever. As a matter of fact, the reason they complain is because they want someone to tell them that everything is fine. If they get this reassurance they will interpret it to mean, "I have nothing to worry about.") A third and final basic illusion I would like to mention is the belief that one's life is largely due to circumstances beyond one's control. Of course, "successful" people will usually protest that they have taken advantage of good fortune or that they have made their own luck. But in truth, very few people take *basic* responsibility for their own lives.

The point of this too brief discussion on basic illusions is that anniversaries, birthday celebrations, wedding anniversaries and retirement, etc., have a way of loosening our grip on the fundamental assumptions upon which we have based our lives. The difference between a brief and appropriate grief as we say goodbye to an old and trusted fantasy, and depression is our ability and willingness to face these ideas and talk about them. Since I have made this kind of statement several times throughout the book, let me make it absolutely clear that I see very little value in mere expression. Getting "in touch" with one's feelings may hold some temporary relief for a person who tends to keep emotions bottled up. But it will not cure depression and it will never turn depression into an avenue of growth. It helps to share your emotions only if in doing so you find genuine understanding and companionship. *Expression and sharing is only helpful if the fear of separation and loneliness which loss always entails is over-*

come. Regression, a negative identification (becoming like your rejections) with those who have deprived us, and the self-criticism that follows can be avoided only when fear is laid to rest by a sincere response based on an understanding of emotional facts. "Stroking," comforting words and pats on the back may be soothing for a while, but they are basically insulting.

Marriage celebrations, reunions, and graduations are also events which, from the standpoint of depression, have much more internal significance than is suggested by the appropriate and reasonable gaiety which surrounds them. In their own way, each of these events is a memorial. They are reminders of the past; reminders that there is a past that can never be relived, recaptured or redone. It is customary to accept these events with joy and that's the way it should be, but people do indeed cry at weddings, find themselves nostalgically sad at reunions, and at graduations suddenly become possessed of an almost frightening realization that the past of which they have complained was indeed very, very good.

Sadness, nostalgia and a flash of fear are not to be confused with the hatred of oneself so typical of depression. We only hate ourselves if we are not prepared to accept the painful emotions that are part of anniversaries. Since there is no way that we can stop time, no way that we can avoid the oncoming anniversaries of life, we cannot escape the dark side of these joyous occasions. But if we are willing to realize that there is a dark side, then these occasions can be times of a deeper realization of what we are. They can bring us closer to an acceptance of all that we are and they can, thereby, give us an opportunity to live richer, less guarded and more open lives. They can be times of growth.

Anniversaries are occasions when we are made acutely aware of the fact that a significant part of our life has been lived and has become part of our own past and part of the world's forgotten history. I have no desire to deny the joyful aspect of these occasions. There is much to be joyful about, but often our pleasure is unnecessarily blemished by a depressing obligation to deny the sense of loss and separation we quite naturally feel at these times. Hence, we cannot accept the newness of life that anniversaries usher in.

At other times, in other places, the loss involved in anniversaries was not so forcibly denied. But then people in other times and at other places did not live in our happiness-oriented culture. We are not very capable of dealing with depression that is a natural part of living. As a matter of fact, one of the difficulties that I have encountered in writing this book is the problem of talking about depression as a natural part of life without sounding as if I am throwing cold water on fun and games. I take for granted that pleasure and happiness associated with anniversaries and with life itself are unquestionably good. Sex, baseball games, classical music, a biblical sermon, growing zinnias, skinny-dipping, and money-making are fine examples of legitimate, good pleasure. I am all in favor of all of the ways that mankind has invented to increase the happiness of life without hurting others. When I say that we live in a happiness-oriented culture I am referring to the social conviction that if one will live life in a particular way life will just "naturally" be happy.

People disagree on just what kind of orientation will produce the happy life, but everybody seems convinced that unhappiness is unnatural and depression is a synonym for mental illness. Some people are devoted to the religious life, some to a life of material luxury, some to the development of the mind while still others are devoted to the anesthetic happiness of spiritual oblivion. The means by which a persistent state of happiness is pursued vary greatly, but most people in our society seem absorbed by the notion that happiness is not only possible but one of the unalienable rights of mankind. The pursuit of happiness may indeed be an unalienable right, but somewhere in one's life there should be a time and a place to wonder if perhaps the pursuit itself may indeed destroy the sought-after happiness.

Paradoxically, people who are devoted to the naturalness of consistent happiness inevitably end up with a great deal of truly unnecessary unhappiness. When one is locked into happiness as a right and natural state in which to exist, one must artificially exclude unhappiness and in order to exclude unhappiness one must live a lie much of the time. When we lie to ourselves we cease to be a trustworthy loving companion to ourselves. Self-deception is every bit as destructive as the deception of others. The only difference is that when we let ourselves down the result is anger with ourselves, i.e. depression, rather than an angry reproach from someone else.

There was a time when the happiness orientation to life was almost entirely a secular phenomenon. Then as now the secular world sought the simplistic security of a unipolar orientation. It was not easy to stand the ambiguities and fluctuations of life as it really was, so people understandably held on to happiness as the stabilizing "good" of life. Grand philosophies as well as lowly conglomerations of prejudice and ignorance supported the cause at one time or another. Both material wealth and psychological poverty have been proclaimed the royal road to happiness.

In recent years, however, the happiness cult has made significant inroads into the religious world. The Judeo-Christian faith which has for centuries been the Western World's most reliable support in dealing with the tragedy and pain of life as well as the joy inherent in life, seems to be moving toward a disavowal of the basic realities of human nature in order to conform to the happiness philosophy of the secular world. There are in fact segments of the church which seem intent on amalgamating theology which has evolved from the experience of thousands of years with the reassuring (but essentially depreciating) notion that mankind was created to be "OK," "a winner," and "beautiful." In so doing, depression that is an essential part of life is successfully denied but in the process of denial faith is rendered artificial and untrustworthy. Faith ceases to be a vehicle of growth when it is used as a means by which we deny ourselves to ourselves. The god of such a faith can never be a companion to us when life takes us through moments of painful self-discovery. Thus, *ultimate* alienation and despair are assured.

By this time the reader is aware that I have resisted giving lists of things to do at the end of each chapter. I have resisted this because I want you to grasp the basic principles that are set forth in each chapter and make your own application. But if I were to suggest any one thing that one might do in order to creatively accept the kind of depression which is so natural to an anniversary, I would simply suggest that one read the Bible. Don't just read favorite verses, but read any book in the Bible, read about any character in the Bible, take up any subject or any idea and see how soon you come across the simple fact that people from Abraham to Jesus to Paul grew in psychological stature only as they found in God a companion who did not fail them when their life took them through periods of alienation, loneliness, failure and hopelessness. God was not close to them because they were cheerful, happy people. They did not find growth in adversity because they were on top of things. And of course, as any reader of the Bible knows, the progenitors of our faith were not always faithful. They like us tried to rationalize away those dark and loathsome aspects of human nature which time inevitably lays bare. But they found that irrespective of all the cheerful bravado expressed by merchants of illusion *there is*

something basically stultifying about living life without a reali-
zation of the essential perversity of our nature.

Perhaps original sin is an outmoded theological concept. Certainly the endless guilt and needless acts of penance which the
medievalists attached to this concept are outmoded, but by the
same token I must make it clear that in my experience no one
is more apt to become seriously depressed than people who are
constantly trying to circumvent the raw and painful aspects of
our human nature with a simplistic philosophy, psychology or
theology that denies the realities of our nature. Such people may
successfully avoid the sadness and depression which most of us go
through from time to time, but they will eventually face the depressing fact that they have also avoided the deepening, growing
aspects of life. Having held on to everything, they have no room
for growth. To the Christian reader, all that I have said is sum-
marized by the words, "He suffered and was buried; He de-
scended into hell; And the third day He rose again according to
the Scriptures, And ascended into heaven. . . . " For Christ there
was no ascent without descent. There isn't for us either.

X

Death:
A Terminal Depression
or Transcendent Growth

Growth is not just a matter of emotional insight and intellectual understanding; it is a process. It is a natural process and that makes it transcendent to the efforts of the individual. Growth involves stages of progress which cannot be circumvented, even if one has the intellectual capacity to see beyond them, if the result is to be genuine. Growth is a common process available to all persons who are offered circumstances which arouse an awareness of themselves, and a trustworthy, lasting, and honest relationship with someone who can stand to be loved, hated, rejected, and depended upon while they assist in the birth of a new life. An understanding of the growth process is so centrally important to a wholesome, creative view of death that I would like to illustrate it. It would be easy to draw upon psychoanalytic case material, but since growth is a common, natural process, we can just as easily examine it in non-analytic circumstances.

Several years ago an elderly man asked if he could talk with me about a young friend of his. Since the man was an acquaintance and wanted advice, not psychiatric treatment, we decided to talk over a long Friday afternoon lunch. I knew that my friend was a widower of nearly ten years, and I knew that the young man, Johnny, he wanted to talk with me about had been his companion, yard man and chauffeur for the last several years. I did not know, however, that my friend had recently been told by his doctors that he had cancer and could not possibly live for more than a few more months. When the subject of his imminent death came up in our conversation, he showed neither dismay nor concern. When I asked him why he was so calm about it he merely said, "There'll be time enough to be scared and angry a few months from now, after the pain has started. But right now I want to tell you about Johnny, he's already feeling my death."

As he filled me in on the details of Johnny's life, the reason for his concern became evident. Johnny had been raised by his mother since his father was killed when he was six years old. (He was now eighteen.) He was the youngest, and the only boy, in a family of five. After the death of his father, Johnny seemed to lose heart. He could not remember the incident with any clarity but his mother was sure that he took the whole affair (what little he understood) "right in his stride." He was so little trouble that she felt quite unworried about taking a full time job. But, in fact, his schoolwork went from excellent to mediocre. He lost interest completely in the development of his precocious musical talent, and last but not least, he failed to develop friendships with either boys or girls. His accomplishments were few; he was tired much of the time, angry a lot of the time, and depressed all of the time.

My friend first met Johnny in an all-night restaurant where the boy was a combination dishwasher and waiter. After a month of short, weekly chats, my friend asked the young man if he would like to move in with him and work for him. In exchange for his work around the house he would offer him room and board and the chance to resume his schooling and go back to his piano studies. The young man was interested but hesitant and so a Sunday after church meeting at my friend's apartment was arranged. As it turned out there was no further need for discussion of the subject of his moving in. Intuitively the old man realized that the key to the boy's heart was music. That's why he arranged the visit for early Sunday afternoon. It was Sunday Musicale time and when the young man walked into the apartment someone only a few years older than himself was playing a Chopin etude on the Steinway. The boy was enthralled. For the first time in years his depression lifted; he had a father.

In the years that followed, Johnny never went back to depression. He worked, he studied, he practiced and his admiration for the old man grew steadily. Everybody was happy but unfortunately no one realized that the old man's need for a son and the young man's yearning for a father had fixated their relationship. The young man's life had changed markedly but there were still no girlfriends, no sports, and no rebellion. The old man was too delighted to have found a way to make his closing years meaningful to worry about the shortcomings of the relationship.

Then cancer and certain death struck. Everyone expected the young man to deny the impending death and everyone expected sadness. But no one, least of all the old man, expected Johnny to be filled with bitter reproach. My friend was too wise to be hurt and much too honest to ease the situation by building up false hopes. Yet he was disturbed and he couldn't understand. He couldn't understand the boy's anger, his bitter insistence that the doctors were wrong, that death was unfair.

I tried to point out that while things were infinitely better for

Johnny now that he had been living with my friend, he was in fact still a boy. He felt better because he had found a man who would pick up where his father had left off. But he had never really gotten over his father's death. He had never really grown up. I explained that the next few months would be the most critical time of Johnny's life. Everything depended on his chance to face his unavoidable loss, rage over it, cry about it, hope for a reprieve, experience disillusionment and in the end, come to terms with the loss and give up the man who had brought him back to life. My friend understood but feared that there was not enough time for all of this to happen. He feared that his inevitable preoccupation with his own death would keep him from the task of helping Johnny convert his angry depression to genuine mourning. He knew that he also had much to mourn, much to give up before he would be ready to step into death a stronger, more fully developed person. And so he made me promise that I would look after the boy.

Accordingly, I began to meet weekly with Johnny. At first he wouldn't talk to me. Then he began to talk in terms of denial and finally his rage broke open. When the old man died, Johnny refused to go to the funeral. He was too disillusioned, too hurt and confused to face the fact of death.

In time, Johnny got over the death of his friend, but it took much longer for him to get over his depression and resume his life. The old man, the external loss, could be mourned, but Johnny had to accept an internal loss that caused much more suffering The internal loss was a loss of the precious image of himself that life with the old man had created. Under the aegis of his new "father's" love he had seen himself as a talented, hard-working, adoring son, but when he had to face the father's death he had to recognize selfishness, hatred, and fear in himself. In other words, the external loss was difficult but relatively easy to accept compared to the loss of his incomplete, idealized picture of himself.

Eventually he mourned for himself just as he had mourned the loss of his loved one. Interestingly the one remaining obstacle to this process was guilt. Inhibiting guilt, guilt because one is getting over a loss and going on with life, is not unusual. But Johnny was considerably more open about his guilt than most people are. Most people express a feeling of guilty disloyalty to the lost person. However, Johnny was able to see a kind of protection in his guilt. He could see that being guilty provided him a reliable rationale for holding back from growth. Guilt was like a comforter. He enfolded himself in it whenever the forward thrust of his psychological development took him into new and frightening areas. Guilt was an effective resistance to growth and for a while Johnny clung to it. Finally his depression lifted and a new young man emerged. He went on with his studies and at last he began to make friends. Johnny began to love, and not unexpectedly, he loved with much of the same generosity, compassion and joy that had been characteristic of the loving old man that had befriended him. In loss, he had become the person he had learned to give up. Johnny had known many hours of happiness, but now he experienced joy, joy that wells up from the realization of change. It was the joy of growth.

Because growth is the natural result of truth revealed within the context of an honest relationship based on facts, it has predictable features. It is characterized by a persistent resistance to the unfolding of its various stages. Growth that is manifested in qualitative, lasting change is not the proud accomplishment of private intellectual exercise any more than it is the product of overwrought emotions and spiritual ecstasy. Intellectual involvement is necessary. Emotional expression is vital. But the psychological death of the illusions, loves, hates and guilts of childhood is the most essential precursor to growth.

When Johnny gave up his regressive grip on childhood and faced facts, he made the greatest decision of his life. In depression he hung on to the past. In mourning he began to let go. In mourning each childish hope, each yearning for gratification, every wish that he might avoid fear and frustration and remain a beautiful child forever, was gone over. Each one was raged over and cried over until it was finally let go, i.e. allowed to die. Johnny experienced the death of precisely that part of himself which he had mistakenly imputed to the old man, i.e. his childish and presumptuous superiority to the conflicts of mankind. He lost the golden hope of childhood to which the knowledge of impending death always lays claim.

The idea which I wish to put across is that *we can only understand death as we view it as a special example of many situations common to human life which offer people an unusual opportunity for growth.* It is my conviction that the aura of denial and false hopefulness which we impose on the deathbed is only the converse of the unreal aura of tragedy and gloom which we associate with death. Both are entirely artificial, defensive phenomena aimed at preserving the comfortable but stunting infantile illusions which undergird so much of our modern existence. *The fear of death is the fear of growing.* However strange that may sound to the layman, it is familiar as well as sensible to the analyst. Every successful analytic patient has cried out more than once, "You're killing me, you're taking away everything worthwhile in life." This, the patient proclaims, when in fact the analyst only seeks to lay bare the unfulfillable infantile wishes and the painful fears of childhood that are disguised by the patient's debilitating psychological symptoms. The bitterness and fear which characterize the early stages of dying are often expressed with the same language patients use when they are introduced to growth. Both processes involve personal loss. Hence a patient in the throes of analytic growth may describe their excruciating response to the analyst's interpretations as an agonizing death of hope.

Physical death itself is a perfectly easy experience to get through. Given false hope and false reassurances from friends, clergymen, and physicians in matters of unimportance, and unyielding silence in matters of consequence, most patients can glide untroubled into a state of physical deterioration in which they may remain as refractory to the facts of death as they have been to the facts of life. At this point all concerned may relax because there is nothing more to fear. All that is left is physical death which for most people is only an outward manifestation of an inward condition which has characterized a great deal of their life. Death of this kind is not depressing because there is no real experience of loss. Death like this is a comfort. In this respect, many people spend their lives dying. It is so easy relative to living and growing. Death as it is usually experienced is not frightening. It is the inescapably personal opportunity for growth which death thrusts upon one that is terrifying, because growth involves loss. It is the pain of intimate loss which is inseparably associated with growth that doctors, clergymen, and patients alike seek to avoid.

Any experience that has dynamic growth potential involves some real dying, i.e. a process involving an affirmation of loss. *Approaching physical death is life's greatest single opportunity for utterly personal growth because it is an utterly personal loss.* But here it is important to remember that I am speaking of growth as a process. Growth in death is not a matter of a heroic surrender to the grave any more than it is a matter of stoic reflection and resignation. Clearly, death can be an opportunity for growth which is unsurpassed by any other event because it is the most exquisitely personal moment of anyone's temporal existence. The decision open to men and women in death is to affirm or deny that death is beyond righteousness, retribution, and understanding. When all of these things are given up, then death is our first and last chance to embrace the utter humanness of our condition.

But by the same sign, it is our first and last chance to know that in choosing to affirm the loss demanded by death we are open to growth that amounts to a transformation. And there is also the joy of transformation. It is the passionate joy of gaining in loss that which is lost in gain. The emotion is beyond expression. It is an experience to be understood in sharing. Only in sharing our brother's death are we assured that when we mourn and affirm the final loss of our lifetime, the power of depression can be defeated and we can know in abundance the joy which follows the thousand deaths that accompany everyday living.

Throughout the closing chapters of this book (VII-X) I have talked about the unavoidable nature of depression that is associated with the milestone occasions of life. I realize that this viewpoint may seem to be at variance with a conventional Christian view of life and death. The conflict is liable to be most pronounced when I suggest that death demands that one surrender to hopelessness if death is to be a preparation for psychological renewal. Certainly I would not want to deny the obvious fact that some people approach death with serenity and hope. But I would like to point out that this condition can be claimed by two very different kinds of people. Some people lay claim to peace of mind, by virtue of a life of consistent faithfulness and trust. Others quietly witness to these emotions on a very different basis. They are people who have believed and doubted, loved God and hated God, trusted, withdrawn into self-security and trusted again. In

other words, these are people who have known death and resur
rection many times and are, therefore, able to face physical death
with a sense of expectancy.

Obviously I have no quarrel with people who manage to hang
on to their faith throughout life and keep it intact in death. But
this is not the way men and women of faith grow psychologically.
*For growth is a resisted natural process that is always foreshad-
owed by despair before it moves us on to the joy of change and
the peace of God.*

> The peace of God, it is no peace,
> But strife closed in the sod.
> Yet, brothers, pray for but one thing—
> The marvelous peace of God.

> William A. Percy, 1924